EPIC STORIES FOR KIDS

EXTRAORDINARY WOMEN WHO CHANGED THE WORLD

RIDDLELAND

Copyright 2022 - Riddleland All rights reserved.
The content contained within this book may not be reproduced, duplicated or transmitted without direct written permission from the author or the publisher.

By reading this document, the reader agrees that under no circumstances is the author responsible for any losses, direct or indirect, that are incurred as a result of the use of the information contained within this document, including, but not limited to, errors, omissions, or inaccuracies.

Legal Notice:
This book is copyright protected. It is only for personal use. You cannot amend, distribute, sell, use, quote or paraphrase any part, or the content within this book, without the consent of the author or publisher.

Disclaimer Notice:
Please note the information contained within this document is for educational and entertainment purposes only. All effort has been executed to present accurate, up to date, reliable, complete information. No warranties of any kind are declared or implied. Readers acknowledge that the author is not engaged in the rendering of legal, financial, medical or professional advice. The content within this book has been derived from various sources. Please consult a licensed professional before attempting any techniques outlined in this book.

Designs by Freepik.com

INTRODUCTION		PG. 7
PART I: RULERS		PG. 8
1	Building Consensus: Sophie "Catherine the Great", "Catherine II" Anhalt-Zerbst	PG. 9
2	"Let Them Eat Cake" Marie Antoinette	PG. 11
3	Freedom is Just the Beginning: Benazir Bhutto	PG. 13
4	The Spark of the English Reformation: Anne Boleyn	PG. 15
5	Bankrolling Christopher Columbus: Isabella "Isabella I" of Castile	PG. 18
6	The Self-Serving Empress: Dowager Cixi	PG. 21
7	Puppet Master: Catherine de' Medici	PG. 24
8	The Benchmark: Indira Gandhi	PG. 27
9	The Queen with the Can-Do Attitude: Alexandrina Victoria	PG. 29
10	The Peace-Loving Warrior: Golda Meir	PG. 32
11	Ambitious – and Proud of It: Angela Merkel	PG. 34
12	Doing the Seemingly Impossible – Getting an Audience with Caesar: Cleopatra "Cleopatra" VII Philopator	PG. 36
13	The People's Princess: Diana Frances "Princess Diana" Spencer	PG. 39
14	The Iron Lady: Margaret Thatcher	PG. 41

15 Cleaning Up Someone Else's Mess:
Elizabeth "Queen Elizabeth I", "The Virgin Queen", "Good Queen Bess" Tudor — PG. 43

16 The Intolerant Queen:
Mary "Mary I", "Bloody Mary" Tudor — PG. 46

17 The Advice Seeker:
Elizabeth Alexandra Mary "Queen Elizabeth II" Windsor — PG. 49

PART II: ACTIVISTS — PG. 51

18 Firm, Unwavering Belief:
Joan of Arc — PG. 52

19 Don't Mess with a Tigress:
Maria Bochkareva — PG. 54

20 Wrong is Wrong:
Josephine Butler — PG. 56

21 Serving the Poorest of the Poor and the Richest of the Rich:
Mary Teresa "Mother Teresa" Bojaxhiu — PG. 58

22 Remembering the Forgotten:
Elizabeth Fry — PG. 61

23 A Democratic Communism:
Rosa Luxemburg — PG. 63

24 The Twig Gatherer:
Winnie Mandela — PG. 66

25 Freedom Square:
Wangari Maathai — PG. 68

26 The Queen of Temper Tantrums:
Emmeline Pankhurst — PG. 70

27 Teen Activist:
Greta Thunberg — PG. 73

28 The Peace People:
Betty Williams — PG. 76

PART III: EXPLORERS, SCIENTISTS, BUSINESSWOMEN, AND HEALTHCARE LEADERS — PG. 79

29 She Wanted to Make a Difference:
Elizabeth Garrett Anderson — PG. 80

30 The Doctor's Prescription:
Elizabeth Blackwell — PG. 82

31 Fashion as Self Expression:
Coco Chanel — PG. 84

32 Facing the Unknown:
Marie Curie — PG. 86

33 Photo 51:
Rosalind Franklin — PG. 88

34 An Understanding of Monkey Business:
Jane Goodall — PG. 90

35 Poetical Science:
Ada Lovelace — PG. 93

36 The Lady with the Lamp:
Florence Nightingale — PG. 95

37 Having Each Other's Back:
Mary Read — PG. 98

38 A Business Needs a Conscience:
Anita Roddick — PG. 101

39 See You at the Top:
Junko Tabei — PG. 103

40 The First Woman in Space:
Valentina Tereshkova — PG. 106

PART IV: POETS, ARTISTS, AND PROSE WRITERS — PG. 108

41 Sugarcoating Bitter Medicine:
Jane Austen — PG. 109

42 A Free Being with an Independent Will:
Charlotte Bronte — PG. 111

43 The Mystery, The Woman:
Agatha Christie — PG. 113

44	Your Name Says a Lot: George Eliot	PG. 115
45	A Deadly Game of Hide and Seek: Anne Frank	PG. 118
46	Retaining the Spirit of Childhood: Beatrix Potter	PG. 120
47	Harry Potter and the Train Delay: J.K. Rowling	PG. 122
48	Reach for the Top: Sappho	PG. 124
49	Never Underestimate the Influence of Friends: Mary Shelley	PG. 127
50	She Dared to Put It in Writing: Mary Wollstonecraft	PG. 129
51	We Women Have Something to Say: Virginia Woolf	PG. 131

PART V: ENTERTAINERS AND ATHLETES — PG. 133

52	The Supercalifragilisticexpialidocious Actress: Julie Andrews	PG. 134
53	Tough Emotionally; Tough Physically: Joanna Jędrzejczyk	PG. 136
54	Tennis, Anyone?: Martina Navratilova	PG. 138
55	The Dying Swan: Anna Pavlova	PG. 140

REFERENCES	PG. 142
DID YOU ENJOY THIS BOOK?	PG. 149
OTHER BOOKS BY RIDDLELAND	PG. 150
ABOUT RIDDLELAND	PG. 153

Introduction

> "There is no limit to what we, as women, can accomplish."
> ~ Michelle Obama

Let's play a game. For the next minute, name as many famous women who are not from the United States as you can think of. Ready? Set. Go.

Did you come up with at least 55? Did you name activists, entertainers, athletes, authors, politicians, scientists, inventors, and educators? I am just guessing, but the people on your list are likely in this book. So are several other people that you will recognize once you start to read about them. You will also find some women you have likely never heard of, but who either did extraordinary things or paved the way by being first to do something.

This book contains the names and stories of 55 women outside the United States who made an impact on the world as we know it today. Each story begins with an introductory hook that explains why the woman is relevant and then the narrator proceeds to discuss the woman's life, giving you time to see if you can figure out who it is before the narrator reveals the woman's name at the end. Following the revealing, the woman's own words are given, summing up the chapter, and then a sentence summary is provided of a lesson that can be learned from this woman's life.

The selections are grouped for easy reading, but they do not have to be read in any order. There may be a couple of names you don't know – and a lot of facts that you didn't know about the people you do know, so settle back. Who says history has to be boring?

Part 1
RULERS

1: Building Consensus

Have you ever wanted to get a project done, but it is a project so big that it cannot be done by one person? When it comes to this type of project, you have got to have help. How can you arrange for such help?

One, you could threaten with force. I have seen bullies try this. However, as soon as the bully is not there, the project is not worked on. Two, you could lead by example and see if anybody joins you. (Don't expect them to join you. They may ask what you are doing, but don't expect them to help; most people would rather play than work on a tough project.) Three, you could ask nicely and explain why the project needs to be done. If people understand what the project is and the importance of it, they are much more likely to help.

Sophie had a tough project that she wanted to do, but she could not do it alone. She wanted to become the ruler of Russia. This sounded absurd to even say, for her husband, Peter III was the ruler of Russia. People were used to men being leaders, not women. Although she could command the soldiers to do a lot of things, commanding them to take down the king was not something they were likely to do.

Sophie knew that the only way she was going to be successful was if she got everyone to understand why she was doing it. She explained that her husband beat her terribly – which they had seen. She explained some of her plans of how to make Russia great. The priests and the generals that she had to impress liked what she had to say. She convinced them that she should be the leader, and they assisted her in the coup.

Peter III was thrown in jail, where he died shortly thereafter. Sophie was an autocrat, a dictator, but she used consensus all the same to help get what she wanted. She believed in the Enlightenment and sought to modernize Russia. She believed women should be educated, and she opened schools for girls. Under her guidance, the military expanded into the Middle East, Eastern Europe, and Alaska. She made Russia into a European powerhouse and brought pride back into the nation. Her reign, 1762 – 1796, is the longest for a Russian female ruler in Russia's long history. She created the Golden Age of Russia. Although she was born Sophie Anhalt-Zerbst and was sometimes known as Catherine II, her many accomplishments have led history to refer to her as . . . **Catherine the Great.**

Moral
Build consensus whenever possible.

2: "Let Them Eat Cake"

Do you care what happens to other people?

    Most of us are concerned with one person – ourselves. We care about the grades that we get in school, but we don't always care if the other students are mastering the material. (I am not saying to help them cheat or to simply give them the answers; I am saying to help them really learn the material.) We tend to look out for number one – ourselves; if number one is okay, we don't care too much about what happens to everyone else.

11

Marie had that kind of attitude. Marie was an Austrian princess who had married a French prince; the prince became king, Louis the Sixteenth, and she had become queen. Marie, though, was not concerned with the people she governed; she was focused on her power and acquiring things for herself.

Marie enjoyed spending money on herself. Although she was surrounded by luxuries, the peasants were literally starving. When Marie was told that they were starving and didn't even have bread, she uttered a phrase that translates into English as "Then let them eat cake." Marie, who did not do her own cooking, did not realize that cake required eggs and milk, two things that the average peasant did not have access to. When the peasants realized Marie knew nothing about their lives or lifestyles – and didn't care to learn anything – they lost respect for her. Marie didn't let their lack of respect bother her; she kept on doing what made her happy – spending money on herself.

Marie's statement was one of the inspirations for the French Revolution to go so far as to abolish the monarchy in France. Eventually, the French Revolution led to the peasants revolting and putting both Marie and her husband in jail. If Marie had just been a better steward of public funds, if she had been more open to modern ideas, and if she had worked on behalf of the people she governed, the French Revolution may not have gone so far, and the monarchy might still exist. Although Marie did not know the peasants, they certainly knew her; she was . . . **Marie Antoinette.**

Moral
Help other people whenever you can.

3: Freedom is Just the Beginning

If you had a choice of the superpower of flying or the superpower of being invisible, which would you choose?

Both answers are good answers. The real test is, what will you do with that power once you have it? Will you use it for the benefit of others, or will you use it to be self-serving?

Freedom is a great blessing. Cherish the freedoms that you have. Many people have fought and died for freedom. Freedom, though, is not an end. Freedom is a beginning. Just like flying or being invisible would be a beginning, we must use the gift of freedom wisely.

Benazir lived in turbulent times in Pakistan. Her dad won the first election in Pakistan in 1978, but a year later Pakistan had a military coup – the army rebelled and took over – and he was hung. She took over as the leading figure in the Pakistan People's Party (PPP); democracy was restored, and she was elected Prime Minister of Pakistan in 1988.

She was the first woman to lead a Muslim nation. She was a big believer in democracy. She was defeated at the polls in 1990 but won re-election in 1993. She served as President from 1988-1990 and 1993-1996. She was on the verge of another comeback in 2007, but she was killed by a suicide bomber a few days before the election.

Benazir was a bright light for democracy in a country where many power-hungry people simply wanted to rule. Democracy made her accountable to the people, and, when the people lost their trust in her in 1990 – she was accused of corruption – she gladly stepped aside. Benazir realized she was a female in a traditional male role, and she was not ashamed to be blazing a path for women to follow.

Benazir believed it didn't matter what your gender was, what your religion was, or what your age was – what mattered, was did your policies do what the majority of the people wanted? Being female, being Muslim, and being in her 50s in 2007 were all part of who she was, but those were not where she wanted people to focus. She wanted people to see the policies she represented, and to vote accordingly. If they were going to vote for her, they would have checked the box marked . . . **Benazir Bhutto.**

Moral
Freedom is just the beginning.

4: The Spark of the English Reformation

    We often talk about careers as ladders. People tend to start on the bottom rung and then work their way up. For instance, to be the president of a college, you would first have to be a student teacher, then a teacher, then a dean, and then a college president. Most people climb the rungs; they don't jump rungs. Also, many people don't make the top, but climb as high as they want/can.

    Society in the Middle Ages also had rungs. If you were a woman, the peasant class was at the bottom. A maid was a notch up, but she would wait on royalty. A marchioness was a powerful person, but not as great as a queen. Anne knew these stations in life well and had experienced each.

She and her sister Mary were beautiful girls who had caught the king's eye. The king, King Henry the Eighth of England, was married, but that didn't stop him from flirting with them. Having tired of Mary, the king set his eye on Anne. The king brought her to the palace where she was a maid and then was promoted to marchioness. Anne liked the gifts he gave, but she refused to let him touch her until they were married.

Henry was in love; at least he was in lust. He wrote to the Pope to let him know that he no longer loved his wife; however, the Pope would not grant him his divorce. Henry then declared that his loyalty was with the faith itself, not the Pope, and that the Pope was not over him. He established the Church of England, and, since the Pope had no authority, the Church of England declared that the king never was married; the ceremony that he and his first wife had was just a sham.

Anne married the king as promised. She bore him a daughter, Elizabeth, who would one day become Queen Elizabeth I. Henry, though, wanted a male child to carry on his dynasty. Anne had three miscarriages over the next three years.

It was then that Henry realized Anne was likely never going to produce the heir he wanted, so he sought to get rid of her. He created charges – adultery, witchcraft, and treason. History says that none of the charges were true, but Henry's jury found her guilty. Four days later, she was beheaded.

Henry was already dating Jane Seymour while being married to Anne. With Anne out of the picture, he married Jane, and she gave him a son. The son would inherit the throne, but he was sickly and would not rule long. The throne then went to Mary, the daughter of his first wife. After she passed, the throne went to Elizabeth, Anne's only child.

During her three years as queen, Anne introduced many Enlightenment ideas to the king's court. Just as she had been firm that the king would not touch her until they were married, she was determined to make the country better for all. She is remembered for being the cause of the English Reformation, as well as being a contributor to it. When she accepted death with such ease, knowing she had done nothing to deserve it but knowing she was fulfilling the wishes of the king she served, she became an English heroine. Almost 500 years later, her name is still on people's lips, the name of . . . **Anne Boleyn.**

Moral
Stick with your principles no matter the cost.

5: Bankrolling Christopher Columbus

Projects cost money. If you are going to find a cure for cancer, you are going to have to find someone or some institution to sponsor you – most of us don't have the money lying around to fund it on our own. Similarly, if you are going to start a business, you are going to have to go to a bank, a rich uncle, or someone with money; again, most of us don't have that kind of money lying around.

Christopher Columbus was in need of money. He believed that the world was round – a lot of people believed it was flat – and he wanted to prove it was round by sailing around the world to India, load the ship, and come back to Europe. He had to find somebody who believed in his research enough to fund him.

Having been turned down by three other places - Portugal, Venice, and Genoa, he decided he would ask the Spanish king and queen. Christopher was Italian, but he thought they still might sponsor his work because his research might greatly benefit them. Spain was on the verge of being a powerhouse, and Christopher knew it.

To make Spain a powerhouse, Queen Isabella had married Ferdinand, uniting Spain into a whole. There was no political divide. She tried to ensure there was no religious divide either. Everyone in the country had the Roman Catholic faith; all those with other faiths had been asked to leave. In 1478, Isabella had started the Spanish Inquisition to verify if new converts – particularly Jews and Muslims who had not left Spain - were truly converted. The Pope later decreed Isabella and Ferdinand "the Catholic monarchs". To be a powerhouse, though, the nation still needed a strong economy – and Christopher knew that a shorter trade route meant a stronger economy.

Christopher made his sales pitch, and, to his shock, the king and queen said no. They needed money to fund the army. They kept Christopher in court, though, and, when the army succeeded in its mission, they agreed to fund him. Isabella even stated she would pawn her jewelry if needed. She provided him three ships: the Santa Maria, the Nina, and the Pinta.

Christopher set sail in 1492, thinking it would take three days to get to India. He was wrong about how long it would take. However, Christopher was right about the world being round and it being possible to sail to India by going West instead of East. Christopher, all those with him, and all those in the queen's court thought only water was between Spain and India; they did not realize that North and South America existed. Instead of finding India, Christopher found the New World. He claimed the lands in the name of the king and queen, and soon Spain would be mining in all South and Central America except Brazil and up to Florida in North America. The New World brought both glory and riches to Spain, and Spain would be one of the world's most powerful nations for almost four centuries.

Isabella not only shaped the history of Spain, but also that of England. Her oldest daughter, Catherine of Aragon, married King Henry the Eighth of England. King Henry would later seek to divorce her when she could not bear a son, and this would spark the English Reformation.

Isabella was feared by many and loved by many. History knows her as Queen Isabella the First. Prior to assuming the throne; she was known by the city she was from . . . **Isabella of Castile.**

Moral
If you believe in something enough, you will put everything you have into it.

6: THE SELF-SERVING EMPRESS

Are you smart? How do you know? If you are like most people, you compare yourself to those people around you. If you are above most of them, you answered, "yes;" if you are below most of them, you answered, "no." We frequently compare ourselves to other people. Dowager did that too.

Dowager was the ruler of China from 1861 – 1908. Although she was not the first empress China ever had, her 47 years as ruler made her the longest female ruler in China's history. Dowager had birthed the former emperor a son – the only woman out of numerous women to do so, and, upon the emperor's death, her son was to assume power. Her son, though, was too young, so a council was formed to be the governing body of China. Dowager was not happy with this decision. Dowager wanted power, so she created a coup, and placed herself in charge. She was cold, calculating, and brutal; she stated, "Whoever makes me unhappy for a day, I will make suffer a lifetime."

Between China's Dowager and England's Queen Victoria, women ruled over half of the world. It was only natural, then, that Dowager looked to Victoria to see how she was doing. In Dowager's mind, she was doing excellent. She noticed how she simply gave an order and 400,000,000 people had to follow it; whereas Queen Victoria had to rely upon Parliament. Although they used completely different strategies to retain power, both held onto power until their literal dying day.

Dowager was very self-centered, but that doesn't mean she didn't try to do things for the people. She realized that her country was not modernized like the European countries, and so she sought to bring about changes. For instance, in 1907, she decreed that all women should receive an education. (Of course, these changes were all geared to help her retain her power, but by helping her citizens she was helping herself.) Today she is regarded as one of the most wicked – but also one of the better in terms of progressing her country – rulers in history. Some say she was nicer than history records, claiming her opponents who rose to power after her death and then the Communists who succeeded them painted her in a negative way so people would appreciate them more. Regardless, they wanted us to remember . . . **Dowager Cixi.**

Moral
Compare yourself to yourself and always try to make a better you.

7: Puppet Master

Do you believe everything that you hear on television? Do you believe everything you read? Do you believe everything that is on the Internet? Do you believe everything that advertisers tell you?

Although I want to trust everybody, I know that I cannot. That so-called kid on the Internet who wants to chat with you on your new video game may actually be a middle-aged man. That story about a flying saucer landing in a farm pasture may be a lie by someone who is just seeking attention. Always read things skeptically.

Catherine was one of the greatest manipulators in history. Though her husband and her sons had the title of the king of France, Catherine pulled the strings from behind the scenes throughout their reigns, especially the reigns of her three sons. Most historians believe her sons would not have stayed in power if it had not been for her skillful use of manipulation. She is generally regarded as the most powerful woman in Europe during the 1500s.

Catherine was an Italian girl, but she had connections in high places; her uncle was Pope Clement VII. He arranged that she be married at age fourteen to the French King. The king, though, was in love with someone else, and had little to do with her. She bore the king three sons, all heirs to the throne.

When the king died, her oldest son was fifteen. He was sickly and soon died. Her second son was only ten at that time; Catherine ruled on his behalf from 1560-1563. Her son officially ruled until he passed in 1574. Her third son then assumed the throne. He was still alive when she passed away.

Catherine worked through rumors, innuendo, and suggestions to get her way. She would plant seeds that others would grow into fruition. She was an Italian queen of French people, and therefore not very popular. When she first came to power, she tried to compromise with her opponents, but, seeing that her opponents kept wanting more reform, she soon drew a hard line.

The Protestant Reformation was seeping into France during her tenure. She is credited with having incited the 1572 St. Bartholomew Massacre in which 5,000 to 30,000 Calvinist reformers were killed by Catholic mobs; the plan backfired, however, for, having killed literally thousands of the reformers, Roman Catholicism was known as being barbarous and Protestantism was perceived as the better choice. Despite her efforts to quell Protestantism, rebels grew in strength and the authority of the monarchy diminished.

Catherine tried to manipulate through her image as well. She patronized the arts, believing this brought glory to the monarchy. Patronizing the arts became a signature of French rulers. Although her wickedness may have been exaggerated by Protestant historians, there is no doubt that she was the glue that held together the French kingdom through the reign of three otherwise inept kings. She showed the world that women could rule as well as a man and that they could spin news as well as any male public relations specialist. Although her sons got credit for most of her deeds, historians realize these deeds were usually the result of seeds planted by . . . **Catherine de' Medici.**

Moral
Read skeptically.

8: The Benchmark

My mom has a six-foot picture of a giraffe she keeps tacked on the back of my closet door. In the left margin is a ruler stretching from the bottom to the top. Every six months, she has me stand sock-footed against it and marks how tall I am. She will then put the date beside the mark. It's fun to compare the me of today to the me of six month's ago.

Comparing oneself to one's past self or to other people is a natural thing we humans do. Indira, like me, noticed this. Indira noticed that a lot of women used men as measuring sticks. They compared their wages to men's wages, their time with household chores to men's time with household chores, and even the number of men who sat in the boardroom compared to the number of women who sat in the boardroom. Indira thought that was silly. She didn't want women to become the same as men; she wanted women to grow and flourish, becoming themselves, and thereby becoming something greater than they ever could just being equal to a man.

Indira was the first female – and only female as of the publishing of this book – Prime Minister of India. She served from 1966 – 1977 and again from 1980 – 1984 when one of her bodyguards assassinated her. Indira was the leader of the Indian National Congress political party. Political roots ran deep in her family; she was the granddaughter of Jawaharlal Nehru, a leader in establishing India as a nation instead of a British colony; Nehru was the first Prime Minister of India from 1947 – 1967. Indira often traveled with him and served as his assistant.

Under Indira's guidance, India became a regional power in southwest Asia. Indira oversaw the creation of the new nation Bangladesh carved from East Pakistan but suspended civil liberties and free press when other parts of the country tried to rebel in the lands she directly governed. She lost the 1977 election because of her harsh tactics, but, in 1980, the people realized she was better than the alternative. She still refused to consider Sikh independence, and they eventually infiltrated her bodyguards and assassinated her.

Indira knew that most politicians were males; but she had no interest in being compared to men. She believed she knew what was best for India, and she pursued it. Although she did not set out to be one, she actually became a benchmark herself, a person who other female world leaders could compare themselves to. If these female leaders wanted to know how they were doing, they could compare their record to the record of . . . **Indira Gandhi.**

Moral
Don't always compare yourself to others; feel free to be yourself.

9: THE QUEEN WITH THE CAN-DO ATTITUDE

Have you ever been asked to do something you do not know how to do? What did you do in that case? You had several choices. One, you could have tried it with what little knowledge you had; the result would likely not have been good. Two, you could have declared that you didn't know how to do it and simply not do it. Three, you could have asked for help, got the training needed, and done the job right.

One's attitude is more important than one's skill level. If a person really wants to do something, the person can always learn. On the other hand, even if the person has the skill to do the job, if the person does not want to do the job, the chances are it will not be done.

Alexandrina inherited the throne of the United Kingdom of Great Britain and Ireland (and later became known as the Empress of India as well) when she was 18-years-old. She realized that she did not know everything. However, she was willing to learn. In an era where men sought to keep women from leadership, Alexandrina learned about her kingdom so she could rule it wisely and not rely exclusively on advisors. She ended up reigning for 63 years, the longest reign ever for a queen until Queen Elizabeth II. Alexandrina's reign is known as the Victorian Era.

During her reign, the United Kingdom became a global empire and a major military power. She was very comfortable with technological change, and under her leadership the railways and communications prospered. Alexandrina had her popularity go up and down during her reign, but she started as highly popular when first introduced at age 18 and ended the same way at age 83. A lot of monarchies fell during her reign, but she kept the English monarchy intact.

As queen, Alexandrina didn't go by her first name. Instead, she went by her middle name, Victoria. Therefore, you likely know Alexandrina Victoria of Kent as . . . **Queen Victoria.**

Moral
Your attitude determines your success.

10: The Peace-Loving Warrior

Have you ever had to deal with a bully who wants to pick a fight with you?

If you are ever cornered by a bully, do not hit the bully first. If you do, you can be accused of being the one who started the fight. Ideally, nobody hits anybody, but should the bully strike you, hopefully your friends will be right there to make the bully back off.

Golda faced the kind of bully that corners you and offers you little choice but to fight back, but instead of hitting the bully first, she was willing to take the blow to show that she did not want to fight. Her bully, though, wasn't a person; it was an army. Golda was the fourth Prime Minister of Israel; she was its first female leader. Syrians and Egyptians had gathered on her country's borders, and it was obvious to her that they planned to attack. Rather than attack first so that she could avoid an attack on her country, she was willing to let them attack as proof that they were indeed hostile.

Golda was under the impression that the United States would immediately step into the fray to end it. When the United States hesitated, she pulled no punches. She stated, "If we have to have a choice between being dead and pitied, and being alive with a bad image, we'd rather be alive and have the bad image." She quickly had the Syrian and Egyptian armies in retreat. The conflict raged from October 6 – 25, 1973, and is known by a variety of titles - the Ramadan War, October War, Yom Kippur War and the 1973 Arab-Israeli War.

Golda wanted a lasting peace: "We say peace and the echo comes back from the other side, war. We don't want wars even when we win." She believed the peace would only come when the Arab people respected their own people's lives more than they hated Israel. The 1973 War showed the Arabs the high cost of hate, and the war paved the way for a peace with Egypt. She retired from politics in 1974 and died in 1978, so she did not get to see the 1979 Egypt-Israel Peace Agreement. To this day, however, Syria has not made peace with Israel and still claims to want to wipe the country off the map.

Golda was a peace-loving, straight-talking leader who was willing to do whatever needed to be done. When asked if women were better leaders than men, she simply replied, "I don't see how they could be any worse." Both the Middle East and women's rights movement as we know them today were shaped by . . . **Golda Meir.**

Moral
Don't rule out the possibility that the people who don't like you won't one day be your friend.

11: Ambitious – and Proud of It

Do you push yourself for excellence? Do you challenge yourself to be the best that you can be?

There is nothing wrong with ambition. Ambition can become wrong when you deliberately hurt others to get your way or if you think only of yourself and not the good of the team; but ambition – the desire to get ahead – is not wrong.

Angela has ambition. In 2005, she became the first female Chancellor of Germany – and she was re-elected three times. Her biggest accomplishment, though, is serving as de facto leader of the European Union. (The European Union consists of 27 countries, including Germany, that are primarily in Europe that are united by current political and economic policies; that is like how the United States consists of 50 states primarily in North America.) Under her leadership, the European Union won the Nobel Peace Prize in 2012, and it has begun to emerge as a global superpower.

Forbes Magazine chose Angela for ten straight years – a decade - as the most powerful woman in the world. As leader of both a recently reunited Germany and a recently formed European Union, what she has done is set a precedent in both that will likely be followed for generations to come.

We can't all be leaders of the European Union or Presidents of the United States, but we can all push ourselves to develop our talents to their fullest. Angela was aware of her potential and sought to make the most of it. She had setbacks – she didn't win every election – and she had nay-sayers, but she kept on pushing herself. Whenever you need an example of someone with ambition, think about . . . **Angela Merkel.**

Moral
Push yourself to develop your potential.

12: Doing the Seemingly Impossible – Getting an Audience with Caesar

Did you ever want to get in somewhere that you were not allowed to go? Between kids not wanting to allow you into their clubhouse, sisters telling you to keep out of their room, and parents telling you not to cross the street, I am sure you have. I know I have.

Our house had a crawl space underneath it, and I was told to not go under there. Being me, I was curious about what was under there. I resisted the temptation to disobey my parents. (I realized the rule was for my own good – there might be snakes, poisonous spiders, sharp nails, and a lot of other bad things under there as well as the treasure I wanted to lay my eyes on.) Instead, when my dad had to go under there next, I asked if I could hold the lamp for him. He was more than grateful for the help, and I got to see what was under there. (It was mostly piping and vents, but we did have some boxes in a corner.)

Cleopatra wanted to go somewhere she was not supposed to go – to the throne room of the Roman ruler Caesar. Cleopatra knew about royalty. She had grown up as royalty; her dad was the king of Egypt. When her dad died, she and her twelve-year-old brother became co-rulers of Egypt. Since he was so young, she held the power, even though they were called Queen and King. Her brother listened to some of his power-hungry advisors, and they removed Cleopatra as queen.

Cleopatra wanted to be queen again, and she needed Caesar's help. She knew Caesar had a lot of faults, but she also knew that he could assist her in getting back into power. To get the help she needed would take more than a letter; she had to get a personal visit with him. However, Caesar didn't want to get involved with Egyptian politics or with a female ruler. She was sure, though, that she could change his mind if she could just see him.

Therefore, Cleopatra came up with a plan to get to see Caesar. She found a huge rug and lay down on one end of it. She then had her assistants roll the rug. The rug was then carried by her assistants to the palace. When the palace guards saw the elaborate rug, they thought it was a gift for Caesar, so the guards allowed the group entry into the palace. The guards outside the throne room felt the same way, and again the group was allowed to enter. Once they were in the throne room, Caesar himself demanded that the gift be unwrapped. When they unrolled it, Cleopatra, one of the most beautiful women of the world, was posed on the rug.

Caesar was smitten with her beauty and with her nerve. He agreed to listen to Cleopatra's tale of woe and then agreed to go personally to help her reclaim her destiny. The military adventure went well, and Cleopatra was back on the throne. Caesar, meanwhile, was so enthralled with her, they eventually had a child, Caesarion.

Although this adventure ended well, her next adventure with Roman politics did not. Caesar returned to Rome where he was murdered in a revolt. Caesar's men, led by Anthony and Octavian, crushed the revolt, but then argued among themselves about whether Anthony or Octavian should be the new leader. Soon war broke out. Cleopatra chose to support Anthony, the eventual loser. Octavian, who later went by the name Caesar Augustus, had her put in prison for her disloyalty. She died in prison from a poisonous snake bite. (Mystery surrounds her death – was it pure chance the snake struck her; did she commit suicide by provoking the snake, or did someone toss the snake in there with her? The world may never know.)

You may have heard of Anthony and Cleopatra; William Shakespeare even wrote a play about them. You may never have heard Cleopatra's full name though; it was . . . **Cleopatra "Cleopatra" VII Philopator.**

Moral
No one is perfect, but all people have something to offer.

13: The People's Princess

How would you like to be famous? It sounds fun, doesn't it? Everyone would know your name. You could be a role model for everyone. People would ask for your autograph. People might even swoon as you walked by.

Fame has a dark side, though. One, you get no privacy. People always want to know what you are doing. Two, everything you do becomes public knowledge. Your private life is no longer your private life. Three, people always want to be around you. You have no time for yourself. You don't have time to relax. Four, you become a prisoner in your own house. You can't go outside without mobs of fans waiting to greet you. You must arrange for bodyguards to help you get through the crowd to get to your ride.

Diana experienced both sides of fame. She was the first wife of Queen Elizabeth II's son Charles, the Prince of Wales. Charles was the heir apparent to the British throne. Charles was famous, and when she married him on July 29, 1981, the wedding was shown around the world. Diana was a very likeable person, and people fell in love with the queen of the future.

Diana became the "People's Princess"; they admired her kind spirit. Diana tried to make a difference on a wide range of issues – children, youth, AIDS, and landmine removal. She bore two male heirs, William and Harry.

Diana and Charles had a rocky marriage. In 1992, they separated. In 1996, they divorced. The public got bits and pieces through the tabloids. Through it all, Diana remained popular with the public.

Diana remained very popular, even after she was no longer the apparent queen of the future. On August 31, 1997, she was being driven in a car in Paris. The car was speeding, apparently trying to get away from the tabloid reporters. Supposedly – those conspiracists love that word – the car crashed into the tunnel, killing Diana. (You can believe what you like, but the bottom line is that something happened in that tunnel that took her life.)

Diana's influence continues to be felt today. One way to remember her is to be charitable, just as she was. She didn't want her name to be remembered for the deeds she did, but we remember her name just the same. It was . . . **Diana Frances Spencer.**

Moral
Expect no reward for being kind.

14: The Iron Lady

I don't know about you, but I want to be liked; I don't want people to go around hating me. I am a people-pleaser, and I will try to do what I think people expect of me. For instance, if I know my mom wants me to keep my room clean, I will try to clean it. I like to make her happy.

I feel sorry for a lot of adults; I even feel sorry for my teacher. It seems that no matter what they do, they can't make everybody happy. For instance, the other day my teacher gave us five math problems to do as homework. Some people thought that was too much, and so they were not happy. A couple of the students wanted to do more - can you believe that, and they weren't happy she would only grade five. My teacher did what she thought was best, and I respect that.

41

Margaret had that same type of mentality. Margaret served as the Leader of the Conservative Party in Great Britain from 1975 – 1990 and as the Prime Minister of Great Britain from 1979-1990. She was the first female Prime Minister of Great Britain; she was also the longest-serving Prime Minister of Great Britain in the twentieth century. She showed the world that women could rule just as well as men.

Margaret wanted what she wanted. She knew that some people would think she went too far on an issue and others would think that she did not go far enough; she trusted herself and felt that she was doing it just the way it should be done. Because she was so stubborn and uncompromising, she became known as the Iron Lady. Throughout the 1980s, she was generally considered the most powerful woman in the world.

Working with both Western and Soviet leaders, Margaret guided the world out of the Cold War. When Mikhail Gorbachev offered reforms in the Soviet Union, Margaret was among the first in the West to welcome the news. She even went to the Soviet Union in 1984.

Margaret, though, was no nonsense when it came to war, reclaiming the Falkland Islands from Argentina when Argentina seized them and urging United States President George H. Bush to stand up to Saddam Hussein after Saddam invaded Kuwait. She told George, "This is no time to go wobbly," showing the iron-like determination she was so known for.

Margaret didn't care if she was liked, as long as she was doing what was right. Her steadfastness may have given her the nickname "The Iron Lady", but her parents gave her the name . . . **Margaret Thatcher.**

Moral
You can't please everyone all the time.

15: Cleaning up Someone Else's Mess

Have you ever had something bad happen in your life? Bad things happen. Sometimes we bring them on ourselves because of a silly mistake, but other times they just happen.

I was living in Charleston, South Carolina, a couple of years ago when a hurricane went through. The hurricane caused massive flooding; entire buildings were underwater. We had to evacuate our house because the water kept getting higher and higher.

Eventually, the rivers upstream were no longer getting more stormwater, and so the river gradually started to go back down. It took it several days for the river to get back within its normal banks. Law enforcement was stationed in our area to keep away looters and to make sure that we did not go back prematurely. Eventually, though, the area was declared safe.

You can't undo a disaster – that's one thing I learned that day. You can clean up the mess, you can repurchase materials that were lost, and you can make amends with friends, but you can't undo what just happened. It applied to the flood that day, and it applies to saying mean things every day – once it is done, it can't be undone.

Queen Elizabeth I inherited a mess. She was twenty-five years-old when she assumed the throne of England. Much of the mess had been caused by her half-sister, who had just passed away. Her half sister Mary had earned the nickname Bloody Mary because she had executed around 300 people by burning them at the stake during her five-year reign. Because of this, most people feared and/or hated the monarchy.

Elizabeth could not change the past; what Mary had done could not be undone. She could, though, seek to clean up the mess and make England a great country again – and that's what she set out to do.

Elizabeth understood the pains of the people. She herself had been put in prison for over a year during Mary's reign because Mary thought she might be a Protestant sympathizer. Elizabeth worked to establish an English Protestant Church but also allowed other religions to exist.

Elizabeth's 44 year-reign brought stability to England. Under this stability, England flourished. Francis Drake sailed around the world; William Shakespeare wrote plays and poems that would still be read 500 years later. In 1588, Elizabeth provided the resources that led to the sinking of the 130-ship Spanish Armada, making England the ruler of the seas. People encouraged Elizabeth to get married and to have an heir; she dated a lot, but said that she considered herself married to England, and so she never got married. Elizabeth established England as a sturdy, vibrant nation, and showed that women could rule as well as men. Her subjects called her "Good Queen Bess" and "The Virgin Queen"; other kingdoms called her Queen Elizabeth I, but her birth name was. . . **Elizabeth Tudor.**

Moral
You can't change the past, but you can move into the future.

16: THE INTOLERANT QUEEN

Don't you sometimes wish that all people thought like you did? Sometimes I do. It would save me a lot of time trying to convince them why my way is the right way. Sometimes I wish they'd pass a law saying that my way is the best way and settle the issue. However, it's at that moment that I realize that they have similar feelings. They wish I would shape up and see the world as they see it, and they would like to see a law passed saying that my way of seeing things was against the law. I am glad there is not a law that would require me to say or do something I don't want to do.

I believe in tolerance, but a lot of people in history do not. Take Mary, for instance. Mary was the first queen of England to actually rule the nation – there had been other queens, but they always served with their husbands and he was looked to as the superior leader. Mary had no husband when she came to the throne, and, even when she married Phillip of Spain, she was still looked to as the English leader. Mary believed everyone should worship exactly as she did.

England had been a Roman Catholic country when she was born. Her dad, King Henry the VIII, believed her mother could not provide him a male child, so he sought a divorce. When the Pope did not provide it, the king started the Church of England, which granted him the divorce because he had married his brother's wife. King Henry's second wife didn't bear a male either, but she bore a girl named Elizabeth. As long as there was no male heir, Mary was first in line for the throne because she was the oldest child. King Henry then executed his second wife for treason and married a third; his third wife bore a son, Edward.

When King Henry VIII died, the throne went to Edward. Edward was sickly and had no heirs, so, when he died the throne went to Mary. Edward was Protestant and publicly pleaded for Mary to become Protestant too, but she refused.

Once Mary came to power, she was resolute on returning the country back to the way it was prior to her dad's reformations. She proclaimed the Church of England null, and said that its divorce decree meant nothing – therefore, she was a legitimate child and that the marriage of her mom to the king was not a sham. She insisted that everyone worship as she did, and, if they did not, she executed them, usually by burning them at the stake. She obtained the nickname "Bloody Mary" for her crackdown, and at least 300 people were burned.

Mary married the king of Spain, hoping he could give her a male child to continue her dynasty. He never did. She ruled for five years. When she died, the throne went to her half-sister Elizabeth. Elizabeth promptly put an end to the persecutions. Mary's fans know her as Mary I and her opponents as Bloody Mary, but her true name was . . . **Mary Tudor.**

Moral
Be tolerant of others.

17. The Advice Seeker

Life is one decision after another. As soon as I awake, I am faced with the decision of whether I should get out of bed. The decision making continues until I finally lay down to go to sleep, and even then, I have to decide if I want to be on my left side, right side, back, or stomach.

Most decisions I have to make during the day are fairly basic, and I can make them without too much stress. A few decisions are very, very hard, however. For instance, I may have noticed the new girl in school needs a friend, but my friends have told me that if I make friends with her then they won't be my friends anymore.

For tough decisions, I like to get other people's input. I may ask my parents, my friends, my teacher, my Scout leader, and just about anyone else that I believe might have insight. I listen to what they say, and then I make my decision.

That's what Queen Elizabeth II does too. She realizes that she does not have all the answers, even though she has ruled the United Kingdom and fifteen other commonwealth realms for over 65 years, the longest of any monarch in the kingdom's history. She will find people who are experts on the subject and ask them for their opinions.

You might be surprised to learn that experts don't always agree with each other. One expert may say the economy will grow and another will say that it will shrink. Both are economic experts, but each has a different perspective. When experts don't agree, she has to call in more experts to determine what she should do. Once she has listened to the experts, the decision is hers to make – she has final responsibility.

The same is true when you listen to people too. You can't blame them even if you follow their advice. You also don't have to take the advice that they give, but most of the time, you would be silly not to since they are experts in the field, and you are not. We have to think for ourselves, but we need to base our decisions on wise counsel; that advice comes from the person we call Queen Elizabeth II; her real name is . . . **Elizabeth Alexandra Mary "Queen Elizabeth II" Windsor**

Moral
Seek wise counsel.

Part II
ACTIVISTS

18: Firm, Unwavering Belief

Have you ever flown a kite? To fly a kite, you need to find a good wind. The wind will catch your kite and lift it. (Make sure you have a good string; otherwise, you may be going on a hike to retrieve your kite.) Your kite has no mind of its own; it simply goes wherever the wind takes it – and the wind is very unpredictable.

We need things that we can believe in; otherwise, like that kite, we will go wherever the wind takes us. If we believe in a goal or a cause strong enough, we will pursue it no matter the cost. The winds of change may blow upon us, but we will keep pursuing the goal.

Joan was a 16-year-old girl living in France in 1428. The English were winning the Hundred Years War and were approaching her village. Many in the village had already fled, fearing for their lives. Joan believed in French independence; she believed in it so much that she was willing to die rather than surrender.

Joan had a vision that the French could hold onto the village and reclaim the city of Orleans which the British had under siege. Joan shared her vision with the French king. His advisors thought she was crazy, but the king listened to her and provided her with the men she needed.

On the day of the battle, Joan dressed like a man and rode a white horse. She was so confident in her vision that all the men around her were confident too. The British were shocked at the determination and sense of destiny the army had, and the British not only quit advancing but also retreated for Orleans.

One day shortly after that, Joan was riding her horse and fell off. Some French noblemen who were working on behalf of the British – they expected Britain to win the war and they wanted to be high ranking in the new society – saw her fall and captured her. They turned her over to the British. She was charged with witchcraft and with dressing like a man, and they burned her at the stake.

In 1456, the Pope reviewed her case and said that it was not witchcraft; he declared her a martyr, and she has been canonized as a saint. Joan's actions had reinspired the French armies, and France remained an independent nation; because of Joan's visions, France regards her as one of its patron saints. Joan received the nickname "The Maid of Orleans" for her efforts; most people know her better as . . . **Joan of Arc.**

Moral
Be committed to whatever you believe.

19: Don't Mess with a Tigress

Past societies were structured so that the men would go off to war and the women would stay home. You have probably seen scenes on television where the woman is standing in the window weeping as her son or husband leaves the house to prepare to go to war. This structure made sense because women are the ones who have and raise children, and a woman was too precious to risk losing on the battlefield.

Today's wars though are not fought just with male soldiers. Societies have realized that they need every abled body of both genders to hold off an otherwise overwhelming army. In World War I, the Russians were in trouble. Germany was advancing. Maria knew if the Germans were to be stopped, she needed to get to the front to stop them.

Conditions at the battlefront were not for dainty women. The weather was cold and miserable; it was muddy, and there were bullets in the air. The men didn't have time to protect a damsel in distress; they had to focus on keeping the enemy at bay and keeping themselves safe. Maria, though, had experienced a drunken father, two abusive boyfriends, and hard work – she was not going to be a burden, and she could handle the conditions.

Maria was not the only female serving in the military. Most females kept their hair short and looked like males; they didn't want anyone to know they were females. Maria boldly declared that she was a female. At first, the soldiers thought she was a prostitute, but she made it clear she was there to fight for her country. She earned the soldiers' respect in battle. For instance, after one ill-fated attack, she pulled 50 wounded soldiers back to safety in the foxholes even after taking a bullet in the leg.

She persuaded Alexander Kerensky, Russia's military leader, to let her form an all-female squadron. She formed the First Russian Women's Battalion of Death. When the military recruited women to join her squad, over 2,000 volunteered. Knowing the rough conditions ahead, Maria spared them no mercy, and that number fell to 300. After training, the unit went to the Western Front where her unit participated in the Kerensky Offensive.

Maria proved that she and her female soldiers had the courage to fight, had the strength to fight, and had the endurance to fight. She showed Russia and the world that women could serve in the military and be an asset to their country. Sadly, Maria's country was undergoing the Communist Revolution, and, because of her being emboldened to fight for the Russia she loved, the new regime realized she might not like them, and they branded her as "an enemy of the working class." On May 16, 1920, a Russian firing squad executed one of its greatest citizens . . . **Maria Bochkareva.**
Women can fit in the military.

20: Wrong is Wrong

Do you get upset when you perceive that your parents have double-standards; that is, they have one set of rules for you and another set for your sister? For instance, perhaps when she stacks salt and pepper shakers on top of each other, they say that it's cute; but when you do it, they get mad.

English society at the turn of the twentieth century had double-standards too, and Josephine dared to say that having double-standards was wrong. She believed that men and women should get the same pay for doing the same job. (Society defended itself by saying that the woman should stay home and that the man was actually making more money because he had to support two people.) She also said that men should be true to their wives if they expected their wives to be true to them, for many men were not being true to their wives. She expected people to practice what they preached.

Josephine often found people not practicing what they preached. For instance, she knew many in the Parliament publicly supported doing away with child prostitution. (Sadly, in the 1800s parents often rented their children to men who would abuse them. Child slave rings also operated in England, selling girls to the continent.) One day, though, when she went to personally retrieve a twelve-year-old girl who had been given to a brothel, she entered the brothel and found several members of Parliament inside. She immediately gave them a lecture about how their deeds should match their words, and the embarrassed men slinked away, hopefully to never do it again.

Josephine worked with the legislature to pass laws regarding selling one's child, upping the age of consent, and outlawing child prostitution. Josephine promoted human dignity for those women who were prostitutes, successfully repealing a law that gave the police the right to search a woman just because they thought she might be a prostitute. Josephine promoted education for all women. She wrote many pieces regarding women's rights, the most famous being the 1896 *Personal Reminiscences of a Great Crusade*.

I realize that some child-selling still goes on secretly in society – I see billboard posters in my town telling us to be on the watch for it. However, it is something that now happens to very few children instead of to many – and something you may not have even thought about until you read this biography, and we owe our peace of mind to . . . **Josephine Butler.**

Moral
If it's wrong, it's wrong.

21: SERVING THE POOREST OF THE POOR AND THE RICHEST OF THE RICH

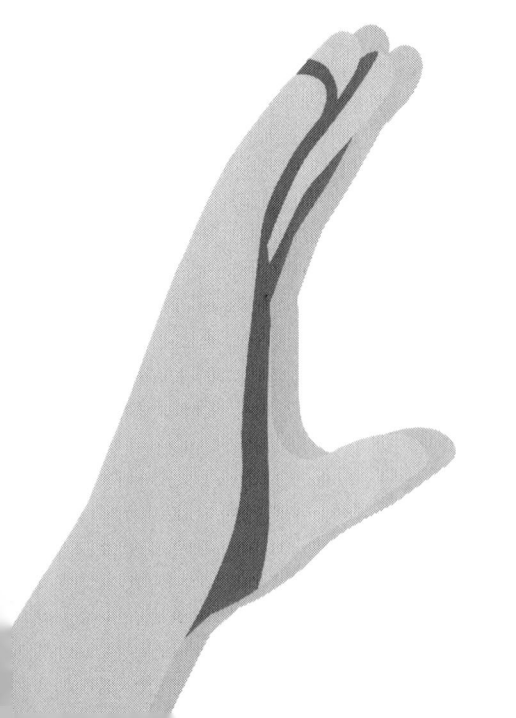

Do you like to help people? I do.

Who are you most likely to help? Are you more likely to want to mow the yard of the rich man or go to the shelter to serve dinner to the poor man? If you are like most people, you picked the rich man. The rich man likely smells nicer, and he is likely to reward you for your effort. The poor man can't help how he smells, and he has no means to reward you, except perhaps a smile. Teresa, a famous nun, taught that we should help both of them. Rich or poor should not matter; whether they can benefit the one who helps them in the future should not matter. If they need help, we should be willing to help.

Teresa described herself the following way, "By blood, I am Albanian. By citizen, an Indian. By faith, I am a Catholic nun. As to my calling, I belong to the world. As to my heart, I belong entirely to the Heart of Jesus." She was a nun who worked in Calcutta, India, among the poorest of the poor.

Not only did Teresa do hands-on work in India, she also founded the Missionaries of Charity, a Roman Catholic organization. The organization is active in over 130 countries, managing homes to comfort those dying of leprosy, HIV/AIDS, and tuberculosis; soup kitchens; mobile clinics; orphanages; schools; and family counseling. A work force of 4,500 nuns work on the organization's behalf. Teresa insisted that all people should have access to the services, regardless of whether they could pay for them.

For her work, Teresa won the Nobel Peace Prize in 1979 and became an example of compassion for the world, regardless of one's religious beliefs. You may never have heard of Mary Teresa Bojaxhiu, but you likely have heard of . . . **Mother Teresa.**

Moral
Help anyone you can – even if they can do nothing in return.

22: Remembering the Forgotten

Have you ever gotten in trouble? I have to admit that I have. I have experienced a wide variety of punishments. I have had to stand with my nose in the corner, write "I will not talk in class" over and over, and even run extra laps.

What is the purpose of punishment? Is it to get revenge on the person who did the bad act? Is it to help the person who did the bad act to think about what they did? Is it to give the person time to cool down so no more bad decisions are made? These are questions that not only teachers and parents have to ask, but so do societies.

Most English people in the early 1800s did not ask these questions. For them, prisoners were out of sight and out of mind. Betsy was different. Stirred by her Christian beliefs, she thought that prison should be a humane place. She encouraged people to ask if they or a close relative were in prison, how would they want prisoners to be treated. Betsy believed the purpose of prison was to reform the criminal so the criminal could become a productive member of society. Prison was not meant to be a final destination; it was a place for rehabilitation.

Betsy was a social worker as well. When she saw a boy homeless on the street, she sought to create a shelter for the homeless. The slave trade was still going on, and she vocally opposed it. Betsy inspired others to get behind the causes and strive to make a better society.

Queen Victoria heard of Betsy's work and met with her in person several times. The queen also funded some of Betsy's charities. Betsy's humanitarian efforts also had admirers in Parliament. Her admirers were able to pass laws to clean up prisons, but, unfortunately, no funds were available to perform inspections; therefore, these laws changed very little in society. Betsy's work, though, led to the social worker movement which continues to this day.

Betsy was chosen as one of the social reformers honored on a commemorative stamp in 1976. Beginning in 2001 and running until 2016, Betsy appeared on the reverse side of five-pound notes issued by the Bank of England. The note showed her at Newgate Prison reading to prisoners. If you have a five-pound note printed between 2001 and 2016, turn it over and you will see a picture of . . . **Elizabeth Fry.**

Moral
Prison is meant to reform.

23: A DEMOCRATIC COMMUNISM

Do you love to tell jokes? I do. One of my favorite types of jokes is what do you get if you cross a (fill in the blank) with a (fill in the blank)? For instance, what do you get if you cross a lawn mower with a cow? Answer: A lawnmoooooer.

Some people try to mix things in real life. We hear about scientists doing it. Did you know that philosophers do it too? For instance, Rosa tried to mix communism with democracy.

Rosa was born in Poland when it was still part of Russia. She went to college in Switzerland where she met her husband. They settled into Berlin, Germany, and at age 28, she became a German citizen.

Rosa was a strong believer in communism. While in school in Russia, she engaged in some revolutionary activities, as did many of the students. These little acts were preludes to the First Russian Revolution – a time of military mutiny, peasant unrest, and worker strikes – which would take place in 1905. While attending college, she established what would become the Polish Communist Party.

Rosa valued the working class. She looked forward to a day in which everyone was equal. She believed that democracy was a part of communism. She believed in free speech; she claimed that everyone had a right to be heard. She was for the free press because this was a place where ideas could be shared. She believed that her brand of communism should be worldwide and should not be merely a system by which to govern a country.

Rosa strongly opposed World War I. She believed the world should unify under communism, and that nationalism was keeping the global communist revolution from happening. After the war ended, discontent in Germany was high. Rosa recruited numerous workers to the Communist Party of Germany, and it looked like Germany could become the utopia she envisioned. Somebody, though, got in a hurry, and things spiraled out of control. Between January 5-12, 1919, workers struck and tried to create a revolution such as Russia had undergone. Rosa was against the timing but supported the movement. The movement was put down, and Rosa, perceived as an instigator, was executed when a German soldier burst into her home and shot her.

Rosa gained celebrity status after World War II. When World War II ended, the Russians had received one-quarter of Berlin and all East Germany. (The British, United States, and French got the other quarters of Berlin.) During the Cold War, the Russians reminded Germany that communism had been a part of Germany for a long time; they even had an annual holiday to celebrate . . . **Rosa Luxemburg.**

Moral
Value free speech – speak up but be willing to listen to others.

24. The Twig Gatherer

Have you ever taken a twig and snapped it into two parts? It was pretty easy to break, wasn't it? What happened if you held two sticks together and tried to snap them? You were probably still able to break them, but now it was harder. What if you added a third stick and tried to snap it? A lot of people could not snap the pile of three twigs in half. If we added yet another stick, very, very few people could snap it. One stick by itself is powerless, but, when a lot of sticks join together, they can be very strong.

Winnie knew that was how it was with people too. Winnie grew up in South Africa at the time of apartheid. Apartheid was approved in 1948. It was created to ensure that the minority of whites would continue to rule the country. Apartheid broke people into different classes by color, and the color of one's skin dictated what one could and could not do. Whites had the most freedom, then Asians, then mixed races, and lastly blacks. One's skin color determined what jobs one could have, where one could live, and even with whom one could socialize.

Winnie was married to Nelson, an anti-apartheid activist. Her husband was put in jail in 1963 for his anti-apartheid activities and not released until 1990. Winnie, though, made sure that neither he nor his mission were forgotten.

In 1991, apartheid was repealed. In 1994, South Africa had its first election in which every citizen could vote. Nelson was elected President of South Africa. However, Winnie did not become the first lady. Although they had been thought of as the ideal couple while he was in prison, they sought a divorce shortly after his release. Winnie said she had only known him a short time before prison, but, now that she got to know him better, he was not someone she would be happy with. Nelson tried to keep the reasons for seeking the divorce a secret, but word leaked out that Nelson was made aware that she had been with someone else while he was gone.

Although Nelson was the image of the leader the people wanted, Winnie is one who helped to shape his public image. She was proud of that image, and even after the divorce, she kept his last name; she wanted people to call her . . . **Winnie Mandela.**

Moral
United we stand.

25: Freedom Square

Do you like to see new buildings go up? I do. It is fun to see a vacated piece of land become a site for a home or a store. However, there comes a point where we have all the houses and stores that we need in the area, and the land could be better used for a garden or a park.

Wangari knew this. When she heard that they were going to build a skyscraper in a park in her native country of Kenya in 1989, she organized a protest. She dared to defy the country's leader's plans for development. The government found this behavior disturbing; it was unwelcome; it was subversive; and it was not at all appropriate for a woman. Wangari had been arrested and beaten on other occasions, but on this occasion, the government backed down. The spot that she stood on to lead the protest is known as "Freedom Square." She believed that by being persistent – by protesting again, and again, and again – that she would wear down the opposition and get her message of environmentalism across.

Wangari was a very intelligent woman. Most Kenyan women did not go to school, but her dad had sent her to school. She had done so well that she earned a scholarship to attend college in the United States. While in the United States she saw the Civil Rights Movement protests and the anti-Vietnam War protests; she used the leaders' techniques when she returned to her East African nation.

In 2002, the people finally switched leaders. Not only was a new leader of the country elected, Wangari, who had run and lost several times, also won an office in parliament in 2002. The new leader appointed her Assistant Minister of Environment, Natural Resources, and Wildlife. In 2004, her past and current efforts were recognized; she won a Nobel Peace Prize for her work of promoting sustainable development while promoting democracy and peace. She became the first black African woman to win a Nobel Prize.

Wangari was a problem solver who believed in maintaining the environment and in progressing women's rights. Quite often, the two could be done together. For instance, when she noticed an area had no trees, she hired women to plant trees. This provided meaningful employment to the women and provided trees for future generations. In all, she provided 30,000 women with new skills and new opportunities. They planted over 30 million trees, so when the next generation enjoys the shade, beauty, lumber, and everything else a tree can provide, they need to remember to thank . . . **Wangari Maathai.**

Moral
Practice what you preach.

26: The Queen of Temper Tantrums

Have you ever been in a grocery store or department store and watch a child throw a temper tantrum? When the child does not get what the child wants – a box of cereal or a toy – the child will tug on its mom's arm to drag her back. If that doesn't work, the child will fall on the floor, bang on it with its fists, yell and cry.

Parents react in different ways to this. Some will immediately scoop up their child and walk out of the store. Some will ignore it and keep shopping. Many will give in to the child's demands in exchange for the child not continuing the tantrum.

Emmeline knew the temper tantrum approach often worked. By making so much noise, one could not be denied. Therefore, when she wanted society to provide English women voting rights, she did not just carry a picket sign and stand out of the way– she made sure that people noticed her.

Emmeline founded the Women's Social and Political Union (WSPU) in 1903. Unlike other groups which simply picketed or wrote letters to the newspaper editor to argue the cause, her organization believed in action. When police officers came to tell them to move along, they would attack the officers. They vandalized as well, smashing store windows so that they could not be ignored. Emmeline, her two daughters, and her group members were repeatedly arrested for these unruly activities. While in jail, they continued to draw attention to their plight by going on hunger strikes; to keep them alive, the prison staff sometimes had to force feed them to keep them alive. The attention-getting tactics continued to escalate, and Emmeline even adapted arson as a technique. This caused many people – including those who believed in the cause of women having the right to work and the right to vote – to shun her group.

Emmeline didn't care; she had a point to make, and she didn't plan to stop until she got what she wanted. However, when the German's threatened England's independence as World War I began, she stopped the destructive tactics so everyone could focus on keeping the Germans away. She believed in the power of humiliation, and she was so patriotic that she gave white feathers to any man who did not join the military; the White Feather Movement humiliated these men in public for their perceived cowardice.

In 1918 at the end of the war, women ages 30 and up received the right to vote. Men were allowed to vote as young as age 21; the government said the cut-off was at 30 for the women because there were not that many men left following the war deaths, and it believed both genders having equal weight in the final decision. Emmeline wasn't alive to see it, but in July 1928, women, like men, over the age of 21 were granted the right to vote.

Although her tactics were questionable, history recognizes Emmeline as a major force behind the rights for women. Today, a statue of her has been placed in the Victoria Towers next to the House of Parliament so that people will recall her; when a child sees the statue, the child will request, "Tell me about . . . **Emmeline Pankhurst.**"

Moral
Actions sometimes speak louder than words.

27: TEEN ACTIVIST

Don't you hate to be the one who brings bad news? I know I do. Sometimes, though, we have no choice but to share that bad news.

For instance, the other day my sister and I went for a car ride with my dad. We were far from home when my sister remembered that she had left a space heater on and that it was close to the curtains with no one watching it. I didn't want to get her in trouble, but I knew I had to tell my mom. If I didn't tell my mom, our house could literally catch on fire. (Never put a space heater by a curtain, even if you can see it. Never leave a space heater which is turned on unattended.) I didn't want to bear the bad news, but I knew I had to do it.

Greta was a schoolgirl in Switzerland. Like many people, she was one of those people who denied that climate change was a reality. She admitted that if it were a reality, it would be a severe crisis and should be the highest of all priorities. Then one day, she came to believe the climate activists were telling the truth.

Greta was shocked that politicians and people who had the power to do something about climate change were not doing anything. She believed it was the most important issue in the world – future generations depended on it being addressed by the current world leadership. What's even more shocking, she found, is that most of these leaders knew the solution to the problem – they just didn't want to implement the solution because it would inconvenience the people of their nations.

In an effort to literally save the world, Greta became an activist. Her youth, her very detailed comments, and her willingness to bluntly challenge world leaders all drew attention to her, and she became a figurehead for the climate change movement. She staged a strike in which students boycotted school to draw attention to climate change, and she even appeared at gatherings of international leaders – all while being under 17 years of age. Greta has advocated world leaders tell the truth about the climate, even if it will make them unpopular. Ironically, this message has made her name very popular . . . **Greta Thunberg.**

Moral
Stand up for the truth – even when it is not popular.

28: The Peace People

Have you ever approached your mom about something you don't like? I have. For instance, I might tell her that I don't think the plaid pants should go with my outfit. Whenever I do that, she will ask me, "Then what do you think should go with it?" If I can answer the question, she will generally agree, but if I answer," I don't know," then she will answer, "That's what I thought," and insist that I wear what she has chosen.

Society is like that too. Many people can see problems all around them. They gripe, moan, and complain about these problems – but they don't offer a solution. Because they do not offer a solution, the status quo remains. If you are going to complain and you really want to make a difference, you must be willing to propose a solution.

Betty was a full-time receptionist and mother of two children in Northern Ireland in the 1970s. Many people in Ireland wanted to separate from the United Kingdom. Most of the separatists were Roman Catholic aligned with the Pope, and most of the ones who wanted to stay were Protestant, aligned with the Church of Ireland. One day, Betty saw some members of the Irish Republican Army (IRA), the separatist group, commit a crime.

In the past, Betty and others in the neighborhood stayed out of the strife; they simply looked the other way and went about their business. On this particular day, though, Betty was not the only one to see the crime. A British police officer also saw it. When the getaway driver refused to stop, the police officer shot him. The getaway car went out of control, striking a woman and three of her four children as they walked down the sidewalk. Two of the children, one a six-week-old baby, died instantly; the other child and mother died shortly after.

Betty realized that innocent lives were being lost, and she believed that a peaceful settlement could be reached regarding Ireland's self-rule. Therefore, she quit being a bystander and stood up to make her neighborhood safe again. The IRA saw her as a traitor; she did not see herself that way. She organized protest marches and successfully drew the world's attention to the plight of Ireland.

It took a lot of nerve to stand up to both the IRA and the British, but Betty knew that someone had to do it. Literally thousands of people had been like herself, waiting for someone else to take charge to stop the senseless violence. She dared to become the voice, and she and the Peace People, as they were called, filled the streets. Most of the Peace People were mothers like herself, although some men joined as well. The Peace People consisted of both people who wanted independence for Ireland and people who did not; they all agreed that a peaceful resolution could be reached.

Betty, along with the journalist who dared to print her story, received the 1976 Nobel Peace Prize. At the demonstrations she gave out whistles so that if anybody saw a crime, they could draw attention to it; this greatly reduced the IRA activity. At the peace rallies Betty always led the marchers in singing "When Irish Eyes are Smiling," a song all sides related to well. Betty brought peace and stability to a war-torn land. It took almost 30 years, but on July 28, 2005, the IRA and the British formally agreed to work through political and democratic programs to achieve the changes they sought, and the IRA insisted its members lay down their weapons. Both sides knew who to thank for the peace . . . **Betty Williams.**

Moral
Be a part of the solution.

Part III

EXPLORERS, SCIENTISTS, BUSINESSWOMEN, AND HEALTHCARE LEADERS

29: She Wanted to Make a Difference

Does not ever having to work sound fun to you?

I must admit, it does sound appealing. However, many people who have had that opportunity did not like it. Elizabeth was one of those people.

Elizabeth grew up in Suffolk, England. Unlike some women who were forced to stay in the house, her parents allowed her to go to the beach and hang out along the shore. Elizabeth wanted to do something with her life, though, not merely to exist. Her parents did not understand this, and they especially didn't understand when she announced she wanted to be a doctor.

Being a doctor was considered a man's work; England had no female doctors at the time. England had nurses, and people like Florence Nightingale had served valiantly during the Crimean War. Elizabeth didn't want to settle for being a nurse, she wanted all the skills of a doctor.

Elizabeth could not find a school that would accept her, so she hired private tutors. In 1865, she took her medical test and she passed. Being a woman, she was not allowed to practice in the hospital, so she set up a private practice in London. Business was slow at first, but gradually picked up. Later that year, there was an outbreak of cholera that affected both rich and poor people. Being desperate for a doctor, most people were willing to overlook her gender.

Elizabeth was the first female doctor who graduated in England; the second female doctor in England overall. (Elizabeth Blackwell had earned her medical degree in the United States and had come to England to practice.) She was so popular that in 1908, she was elected mayor of Aldeburgh, making her the first female mayor in England. As mayor she spoke out for women's rights. If you were going to vote for Elizabeth, you would want to search the ballot for her full name . . . **Elizabeth Garrett Anderson.**

Moral
Choose a career you will enjoy – and then strive to achieve it.

30: The Doctor's Prescription

Does your mom rearrange the furniture in your living room every few weeks? Mine does. She is looking for the perfect combination of being both functional and beautiful.

Did you know that society can be rearranged too? That's right, the society structures that we have today do not have to be the structures that we have in the future. Many people assume that society has always been this way and that it will always be this way. My grandpa, though, can tell stories about when cell phones did not exist, when most drug stores had soda fountains in them, and when most doctors were men. My grandpa realizes that society has changed a lot, and that our generation may change it some more, either intentionally or accidentally.

Elizabeth, an English girl whose family had migrated to the United States, was one of the few in her generation who realized that society could be changed. Elizabeth grew up in the 1850s in a very male-dominated society, one in which slavery was considered okay. The looming Civil War suggested change regarding slavery was on the way.

Elizabeth wanted another change, though. She wanted women to have the same opportunity as men. In particular, Elizabeth wanted to be a doctor. She had applied to many medical schools, but, once they found out she was a female, they refused her application. Finally, she applied at Geneva Medical College in Geneva, New York, and they agreed that she could attend.

Elizabeth graduated at the very top in her class; she was the first woman to graduate from medical school in the United States. To give other women a chance to be doctors, she opened her own school, New York Infirmary for Women and Children; today that school is a teaching hospital, New York-Presbyterian Lower Manhattan Hospital. She believed most women doctors could offer compassion that many men doctors lacked, and she perceived society had a real need for women doctors.

Elizabeth returned to her native England in July 1869 and set up a private practice there. She also founded a medical training school that paralleled the one she had established in the United States. In 1880, she retired from the medical profession and spent her time traveling and promoting social reform. Today, the medical field gives a medal out annually in her honor to recognize a woman who has deeply impacted the medical field; they call that award the . . . **Elizabeth Blackwell Medal.**

Moral
Never hesitate to remodel if something needs to be remodeled.

31: Fashion as Self-Expression

Are you going to pass your grade this year and move on to the next grade?

If you sincerely believe your answer — whether it was yes (I hope it was) or no, it has a very, very good chance of coming true. The fancy words for this kind of prediction is a "self-fulling prophecy." If you think you can do something, you probably can. You will figure out each step necessary to reach that goal. On the other hand, if you believe that failure is going to happen, you are likely to try half-heartedly (which proves in your mind that you were right when you do fail) or not try at all. Your mind influences how hard you will try, and that determines what happens.

Gabrielle was a French fashion designer and businesswoman. Between World War I and World War II, she introduced sporty, casual styles that were widely accepted and changed the corseted style that was there before. No longer were women dressed as dainty prudes; they were dressed ready for anything. Unlike other fashion designers of her time, Gabrielle believed that fashion was much more than just clothing, and she had lines of jewelry, handbags, and perfumes to complement her clothes. In fact, she often suggested not just a dress, but a complete outfit and accessories. In her opinion, clothes were not something one just wore to keep warm or to protect oneself from injury, but were also a form of self-expression.

World War II brought the Nazi occupation of France, and many people thought that the Nazis used Gabrielle as a spy. She denied it at the time. However, recent declassified documents do show that she had extensive contact with the Nazis and that in 1943 they even wanted her to take a message to Winston Churchill offering a way to end the war.

After the war was over and people had forgotten the scandal associated with her name, she again became a fashion icon. Her Chanel No. 5 remains an iconic perfume to this day, (it is my mom's favorite perfume.) *Time magazine* named her one of the most influential people of the 20th century.

You may never have heard of Gabrielle; that's because she went by a nickname. The name behind her signature perfume Chanel #5 is . . . **Coco Chanel.**

Moral
Believe you can do whatever you set out to do.

32: Facing the Unknown

What scares you?

   Like many kids, I used to be afraid of something under the bed. To assure myself there was nothing under the bed, I would get my flashlight out from my nightstand, turn on the flashlight, and lift the covers. I was prepared to use my flashlight as a club if anything or anyone lunged at me; luckily, nothing ever did. Convinced there was nothing there, I could go to sleep.

When I did not understand exactly what was under the bed, I was scared. However, once I could clearly see what was there, my fear went away. Marie applied this same principle to science. She believed that humans had a great fear of the unknown, but the more that we learned about things around us, the more our fears would lessen.

Marie was born in Poland in 1867 but moved to Paris to get her education. She eventually became a French citizen. Marie was fascinated with the recently discovered field of radiology – x-rays, and she became the first woman to win a Nobel Prize for her work. She later won a second Nobel Prize as well – she and her husband Pierre discovered polonium and radium, making her the only woman to win twice and the only person – male or female – to win in two different scientific fields, physics, and chemistry. In 1906, she became the first female faculty member at the University of Paris.

Marie's principle of seeking to understand something to remove the fear from it can be applied to all of life. She focused on removing people's fear of x-rays, but you can apply the principle of understanding your fear to reduce your fear, no matter what your greatest fear is. Because of her efforts, x-rays are routine today, and few people dread going to have an x-ray done.

Marie's birth name was Marie Sklodowska, but, when she married Pierre Curie, she took his name. Therefore, you likely know her as . . . **Marie Curie.**

Moral
The more you understand the unknown, the more at ease you will be.

33: Photo 51

Have you ever been told that you look like your mom?

That's probably because you do. About half of your genetic code comes from your father and the other half comes from your mother. You therefore have about half of the traits of each.

Each person has a unique genetic code. Parents pass parts of their code through deoxyribonucleic acid, commonly known as DNA, a long molecule. Your DNA determines what you look like, how you will function, and how you will grow. The DNA has the instructions that tell our body what to do.

Rosalind worked in the biophysics department at King's College in London in 1951. She studied DNA fibers with x-rays. She and her student, Raymond Gosling, took pictures of DNA. From the pictures, they made a major discovery – there were two forms of DNA. The first form was fairly well known. The second form was recorded on Photograph 51 on their photo set. At Rosalind's direction, Ray had spent hundreds of hours taking the x-ray exposure of the DNA.

Rosalind was so excited that she showed the picture to a friend, Maurice Wilkins. However, she and Maurice had a quarrel in 1953, and, in anger, Maurice showed the picture to another researcher, James Watson, without her knowledge. Watson and Francis Crick then wrote a paper on the discovery and got the paper published later in 1953; they won a Nobel Prize for the paper in 1962. Although Watson and Crick became known for the DNA find, they did at least give Rosalind credit for the photograph in a footnote.

Rosalind deserved the Nobel Prize, and it wasn't until after her death that the truth began to come out as to what happened. The average person today has not heard of Rosalind and her discovery, but, in time, perhaps everyone will know the name of . . . **Rosalind Franklin.**

Moral
Science is a part of life.

34: AN UNDERSTANDING OF MONKEY BUSINESS

Have you ever tried to make friends with a stray cat?

Stray cats are very distrusting. If you want to be their friend, you are going to have to take the friendship slowly so that you earn their trust. For instance, you might set out a bowl of food for it. After you repeat this for numerous days, the cat will gradually come to anticipate it. Then, as you set the bowl out, you can linger longer and longer. In time, the cat will trust you.

Jane wanted to gain the trust of chimpanzees so that she could get close to them and study them. She went to Africa at age 20, and immediately searched for a group of chimps to observe. The chimps she found would have nothing to do with her – they were scared and ran away when she got close. It was then that Jane realized that she would have to take things very slowly.

Jane discovered where the chimps were eating each morning, and so she made it a point to be there. It took over a year, but they finally got used to her being there and ignored her presence. In two years, they would even come up to her in search of bananas.

Using bananas to attract one chimp at a time, Jane got to know each chimp on a personal level. During the day, she would climb trees and eat what they were eating. The chimps went about their daily lives, and Jane was privileged to see things no human had seen before. She saw their social structure, and realized it was set up on a class system, with the strongest males being the leaders. She saw how chimps could mold a blade of grass into a tool to be used as a spoon; she saw that chimps were not vegetarians as previously thought but would eat meat. She saw how chimps would throw rocks at other chimps. The facts that chimps were tool-using, meat-eating, and war-like were all major discoveries, and Jane became a famous scientist.

Jane also became a celebrity. She made many documentary specials about her life with the animals. The first special, Miss Goodall and the Wild Chimpanzees, aired on both U.S. and English television in 1965. The documentaries showed Jane interacting with the chimpanzees as well as discussing her findings. The documentaries kept her research in front of people, and she became a household name.

Jane used her clout as a scientist to become an animal rights activist. She was appalled at poachers who would simply kill for the sake of a trophy. Jane used her research to show that animals and humans were not very different and argued that humans should respect the animals. She claimed that animals should not be used in research.

Jane broke new ground not just with her research findings but even by the fact that she was a researcher. She showed that women could be skillful researchers. Today, there are many female researchers, and their pioneer was . . . **Jane Goodall.**

Moral
Make the world a better place.

35: Poetical Science

Have you ever had to live in someone's shadow?

I know that my little sister has to live in mine. When she goes into a classroom in our small-town school, the teacher will say, "I remember when your brother was in this class." When she does something, it is often compared to how I did it – "Your brother wasn't very good at math, but you're good at it." She has even tried to make my friends her friends. She's had a hard time being her own person.

Ada had the same problem. Ada was the only child of the famous poet George Byron, known to the world as Lord Byron. (Actually, she was not the only child, but she was the only child not born out of wedlock.) Lord Byron was considered the greatest English poet in the early 1800s. Sadly, Lord Byron separated from his wife one month after Ada was born, and then he left England forever four months later; he died in Greece when she was eight, so she never got to know him.

Ada's mother disliked Lord Byron's morals, and she didn't want Ada to be like him. She believed the poetry had driven Lord Byron to insanity, and she sensed that Ada had his poetic genius. To protect Ada from developing her poetic talent, her mom pushed her to study math. (Ada studied math as her mom suggested, but Ada couldn't help but see math through the eyes of a poet, and she called her way of thinking "poetical science".) Her mom hired a private tutor for her. The tutor saw Ada's genius as well, and in June 1743, she introduced her to the British mathematician Charles Babbage. Charles was working on an "analytical engine"; this invention would later earn him the title of "father of computers".

Charles, like all other mathematicians at the time, was focused on the computer doing calculations. Ada is credited with being the first person to recognize that computers could do more than calculations. She is also credited with having written the first algorithm and is therefore regarded as the first computer programmer.

Ada Byron married William King, and took his last name. You have probably never heard of Ada King, though. That is because William was appointed the Count of Lovelace, and, after that time, Ada went by the name . . . **Ada Lovelace.**

Moral
The more you learn about things, the more you realize that there is a lot more to know.

36: The Lady with the Lamp

When you think of a hospital, what do you think of?

I think of sick people lying in beds in a very sterile environment. That certainly is a very common sight today. It wasn't always.

Florence loved to help people, and she had chosen to go into nursing to do it. Florence was from a very rich family, and her family didn't want her in the hospital environment. Nurses were paid poorly in the mid-1800s, and nursing was considered the work of the lower class – who wants to clean up vomit, poop, blood, and who-knows-what-else? Her parents had a nice man in mind for Florence to marry. He was a wealthy man, and Florence would never have to work a day in her life.

At her parents' request, Florence met the man. She found that they really did have a lot of the same interests and that she did enjoy his company. However, she refused to throw away her dream of nursing. Her parents never did support her decision to be a nurse, but, in 1844, she left for nursing school.

She graduated and went to London. At her first job, she enforced sanitation practices and was made a supervisor within a year. When the Crimean War broke out, she was asked to round up nurses and assist the troops. She picked 34 nurses and set sail.

Once in the city of Constantinople, she found English soldiers lying on the floor of the hospital with bugs crawling on them. Many were dying – not from their injuries – but from the hospital conditions. Supplies such as bandages were low, and even water was being rationed.

Florence had the nurses scrub the hospital literally from floor to ceiling. Every waking moment was spent on patient care and making the hospital better. She provided hands on care – she roamed the hospital even at night to care for the injured, and the soldiers fondly called her "The Lady with the Lamp."

In addition to physical conditions, she focused on dietary needs, and also provided intellectual reading materials, and obtained clean clothes for the wounded. Her practices set the foundation of modern nursing. Her philosophy was, "The very first requirement in a hospital is that it should do the sick no harm." After the war, Florence wrote an 830-page report of what she found and recommendations for improvements, and she gave this report to the Army; the Army realized the validity of these recommendations and made changes.

Today, the seeds that Florence planted have sprung and grown. Our healthcare system may not be perfect, but it is far more sanitary than it might have otherwise been. Our healthcare is also far less costly than it would have been as well. Florence truly cared about people – so much so that she was willing to do without a pampered life because she preferred to assist others. The troops called her "The Angel of Crimea" and "The Lady with the Lamp," but history knows her as . . . **Florence Nightingale.**

Moral
The seeds you plant today may grow with time.

37: Having Each Other's Back

When you think of a pirate, what pops into your mind? A man with a hook? A man with a peg leg? An outlaw who hijacked ships? A thug who demanded toll fees to let ships pass without destroying them? A patriot who fought for his country but did it his way instead of following strict military guidelines? An adventurer who wanted to see distant lands?

What probably doesn't pop into mind is a woman. There were women pirates, though. Some of them even had their own fleet of ships and were in charge of the crew. Female pirates could be found throughout the world - Grace O'Malley was off the coast of Ireland, Ching Shih was in the South China Sea, and Anne Bonny was in the Caribbean.

Anne wasn't the only famous female pirate in the Caribbean; so was Mary. Anne had moved from Ireland to the Bahamas to be with her pirate husband, John Bonny. The Bonny marriage, though, was rocky. One time, John believed twenty-year-old Anne had been seeing other men and he had her charged with adultery and ordered her whipped in public. John "Calico Jack" Rackham, a reformed pirate, had offered to give John Bonny money to spare the whipping, but John Bonny refused to take it. Calico Jack then convinced Anne to run away with him and become a pirate. In a daring move, they stole a ship, and headed out to sea, their fates tied together. Calico Jack returned to what he did best – pirating, and Anne was at his side.

Mary's career path was much more noble. She had disguised herself as a boy and gotten a job onboard a British man-of-war. On the ship, she went by "Mark" instead of "Mary," She had met her husband, a captain, revealed her true gender to him, and settled down in the Netherlands with him running a tavern, the Three Horseshoes. However, when her husband died, she returned to the sea. Europe was at peace, so the need for sailors was low. Therefore, disguised as Mark, she took a ship to the West Indies in search of adventure. The ship, though, was captured by Calico Jack. Unaware that Mary was a woman, Jack offered her and others the opportunity to join him as a pirate rather than face death. Mary agreed.

As they sailed, Mary revealed her gender to Anne, and the two became great friends. With Anne's support and protection, Mary let the crew know that she was a woman. From time to time, Mary and Anne even wore traditional women's clothing, but, when prepared for battle, they always dressed in men's fashion. Calico Jack successfully captured numerous fishing vessels along the Jamaica coastline. When called upon to fight, the two women would stand back-to-back, each holding a pistol in one hand and a machete in the other. They literally had each other's back.

For two months in 1720, Jack, Anne, and Mary ruled the seas, and their fame spread far and wide. (You may not realize it, but they are all recalled in modern culture; for instance, Jack flew a black flag with a skull and two criss-crossing sabers imprinted in white on it, and that is the stereotyped pirate flag used in movies such as *Pirates of the Caribbean*.) A bounty was on Calico Jack's head, so both other pirates and government officials sailed the seas hoping to capture him.

One day Calico Jack had captured a large Spanish ship, and his crew were celebrating that night with alcohol. The crew were so intoxicated that officers from a British government ship were able to go aboard his ship unannounced. Most of Jack's men were in the ship's galley and immediately surrendered. Anne and Mary, who were upstairs relaxing with Jack in the captain's quarters, fought until they were clearly overwhelmed. All the pirates were taken to prison and most sentenced to death. Anne snarled in frustration as the men were led past her, "If you had just fought like men, you wouldn't be hanging like dogs." Anne and Mary, though, both escaped the death penalty. Anne was found to be carrying Jack's baby and Mary was carrying a crew member's child. Mary got a fever and died in prison, but no one knows what happened to Anne; she may have died around that time or she may have made it to America, where she is rumored to have lived until 1782. If she made it to America, she would have told her grandchildren about her days as a pirate and how she ruled the waves with Calico Jack and . . . **Mary Read.**

Moral
Have your teammate's back no matter how tough the circumstances.

38: A Business Needs a Conscience

What is the purpose of business?

    If you said that it is to make money, Anita would disagree with you. Although making money is the reason most companies may go into business, Anita does not believe that should be the reason. She believes people should go into the business for the public good rather than for private gain. In other words, your business is offering a product or a service that the public really needs. Anita believes if businesspeople will focus on meeting public needs, then money to the company will follow.

    Anita, a British businesswoman, founded The Body Shop, a cosmetic company that produced and sold natural beauty products. Anita had a large heart, especially for underprivileged

101

humans and animals. Rather than take advantage of third-world countries, she kept her prices fair. Her company was one of the first to prohibit testing on animals.

Anita believed that business should be the most powerful source in society, more than even religion and government. She believed that business should be conducted ethically, and that people should be able to put their trust in companies. She believed that companies should care for people, and, because they cared, they would be the ones promoting social change, fighting on behalf of the people.

Although Anita had a heart for the environment, part of her environmental stewardship was not planned. Anita encouraged people to send their empty bottles back to her instead of throwing them out; this helped save the environment both in terms of the materials taken to make a new bottle and the cost of the old bottle rotting in the ground. The idea of sending the bottle back for a refill, though, was more practical – she didn't have enough bottles to keep up with the demand.

At its peak in 2004, she was serving over 77 million customers through 1980 stores worldwide. She emphasized trust, and people believed she practiced what she preached; she was the second most trusted brand in the United Kingdom. In March of 2006, L'Oréal purchased her business.

In an age where scandals were common and business and profits were being placed before people, Anita offered a different model. Anita knew she was small – when she opened her first store, she was simply trying to find a way to put food on the table for her two daughters while her husband was away, but she knew she could make a difference – "If you think you are too small to make an impact, try going to sleep with a mosquito." She became a guiding light for others to follow; those that followed her followed in the path of . . . **Anita Roddick.**

Moral
Ethics matter.

39: SEE YOU AT THE TOP

Have you ever been mountain climbing? It is hard work going up the hill. If you are like me, your legs begin to hurt – really hurt. However, when you get to the top of the mountain, that breathtaking view makes it all worthwhile.

Then you see it – another mountain in the distance. A mountain that is even taller than the mountain you are on. However, to get to that mountain you must first descend from the mountain you have climbed. To get to the top will require you to leave the comfortable spot you are in, go into the valley, and then begin the steep, painful climb.

Our goals in life are like mountains. We work hard to accomplish a goal. When we reach that goal, we enjoy the thrill of success, and then we see an even greater goal in the distance. Although the mountains I climb are figurative, Junko climbed real mountains.

Junko was a Japanese mountaineer; she also taught school and wrote books. In 1975, she became the 36th person – and the first woman - to ever reach the top of Mount Everest, the earth's highest mountain. (If you don't recall your geography, Mount Everest is part of the Himalayas and is found on the border of Nepal and China.) In 1992, she also became known for being the first woman to ascend the Seven Summits; that is, she climbed the highest mountain on each of the seven continents.

These were not easy climbs. In addition to knowing how to climb and having the physical ability to climb, she also had to have the willpower to climb. No one would have blamed her for giving up; some of those mountains are very steep and very dangerous to climb. However, she set her mind to it, and she did it. She became an example of how, if someone will stick with something, they can go far. When you are thinking about quitting, remind yourself why you started for the top of the mountain in the first place, and then think about sticking it out, just like . . . **Junko Tabei.**

Moral
Mountain climbing is not easy, but if you stick with it you will get to the top.

40: The First Woman in Space

Researchers like to do experiments in which they can compare two groups of people who are alike in every way except one and then try to make the case that the single difference explains any difference they find. For instance, a researcher might test your class and another class to make sure the two classes were equal regarding their knowledge of space flight. Seeing that they were equal, the researcher would give your class a lesson about outer space, and then the researcher would retest both classes. Any differences between the two classes should be due to the training. If the training worked, your class should do a lot better on the test than the other class.

In 1963, the Soviet Union wanted to run a test like that. They wanted to see if space travel impacted men and women differently. They found two cosmonauts – one male, Valery Bykovsky, and one female, Valentina, and made sure the two were equally trained. On June 16, 1963, they put the male on a spaceship, Vostok 5, and placed Valentina on an identical spaceship, Vostok 6. This was going to be a solo mission for each of them – Valentina was going to be the first woman in space, and, to this day, she is also the only woman to have flown a solo space mission.

The blastoff went well. Valentina spent 2 days, 22 hours, and 50 minutes (almost three days) in space. She went around the earth 48 times. When her spaceship reentered the earth, she parachuted about 4 miles above the earth as planned and then drifted to safety. Her male counterpart returned safely as well. Both were hailed as heroes.

Going into space now is so common that sometimes it does not make the front-page news. In 1963, going into space was a major ordeal. Valentina risked her life, not knowing what would happen. She reported feeling motion-sick, but otherwise was okay. Upon returning to earth, both she and her male counterpart were both in great condition. Valentina was willing to put her body at risk so that other women could go into space and not experience any problems that might afflict her. She was a national hero to the Soviet Union, but what she did impacted women – and men – worldwide. (Universe-wide, if you want to get technical.) One day when you get into a spacecraft, think about the pioneers who made it possible, and, in particular, think about . . . **Valentina Tereshkova.**

Moral
Treat the Earth with respect.

107

Part IV

POETS, ARTISTS, AND PROSE WRITERS

41: Sugarcoating Bitter Medicine

Do you like to take medicine?

I don't. Most medicine tastes bad. My mom knows, though, that I need to take the medicines the doctor has ordered. To make the medicine taste a little better, she will put sugar on the bottom of the spoon and then pour on the medicine, and have me swallow it, sugar and all. The sugar helps the bitter medicine to taste better.

Jane knew that her English society had some bitter medicine it needed to swallow. She could see how women used men to obtain social status, and she could see how men used women as an accessory to go with their outfit. She didn't think this was the way love should be.

Rather than write a harsh essay about how people should not manipulate each other or use each other merely as objects, she wrote stories. In these stories, she told stories of romance, and, through both the characters' actions and the characters' words, she made her points. If she had written a blunt essay, no one would have paid any attention, but, because she candy-coated the message with the story, people read it willingly. Some people still read her story simply to enjoy a good story, but today many read it for its historical value: her writings were some of the first to be created in the feminist movement.

The issues Jane covered are something people are still dealing with today, and her books have remained popular over 200 years. Among her writings are *Sense and Sensibility, Pride and Prejudice, Mansfield Park,* and *Emma*; all were first published anonymously between 1811-1816. (In those days, women were not recognized as authors, and, to get something published as a woman almost always meant to do it anonymously or with a male penname.)

Because the books were anonymous, Jane did not get rich or famous in her lifetime. Today, though, she is a household name and many of her books have been turned into movies. That household name, in case you haven't figured it out, is . . . **Jane Austen.**

Moral
Say what you need to say but, if you want people to listen to you, say it in a way that does not upset your audience.

42: A Free Being with an Independent Will

Do you have a pair of sunglasses? I do, (I look good in them too.) Have you ever noticed how sunglasses put a filter in front of your eyes? My sunglasses have a greenish tint, so, when I wear them, everything looks a little greener than usual. The reality I am seeing is slightly skewed; everything looks greener than it really is. People around me don't have my glasses, so my view of reality looks different than what the people around me are seeing.

In life, everybody, in a sense, has sunglasses on. We all see the world differently. We have had different experiences, grown up with different people, and have different talents. We are not alike, even though we may attend the same school or live in the same family.

Currer Bell liked to write romance stories, those stories in which boy meets girl, boy does something stupid and almost loses girl, and then boy and girl live happily ever after. Her stories are a little deeper than that, but you know what I mean, don't you? It's that mushy-gushy stuff.

Currer didn't tell the romance story the way it was usually told, though. In *Jane Eyre: An Autobiography*, also titled simply *Jane Eyre*, Currer told it through the eyes of a character, a character who was often unaware that the reality that she was seeing was not the reality that everyone else was seeing. An autobiography is a true story about oneself, and so *Jane Eyre* is telling her story in her own words.

Jane Eyre broke new ground in literature, and many writers after Currer also told stories with unreliable narrators. *Jane Eyre* is considered one of the great romance stories of all time. I like it, because it makes me think about my own life and writing down my adventures for people to read.

Currer realized that all people were independent thinkers, and everyone saw reality differently. Currer also realized that women were not supposed to be independent thinkers in many cases; they were simply supposed to nod in agreement with their husbands. Currer Bell, as you might have guessed, was not the author's real name. The author had chosen to write as Currer Bell because it sounded like a masculine name and because the initials of C. B. were the initials of her real name . . . **Charlotte Bronte.**

Moral
Everyone sees the world differently.

43: The Mystery, The Woman

Do you love a mystery? I do. At my house, it seems like we are always working on The Case of the Disappearing Television Remote. To solve the mystery and find the remote, I have to ask each person when they saw it last and where it was; sometimes I have to re-interview somebody because they had a "Oh, yeah, I forgot" moment. I then put the clues together, determine where it was last seen, and then determine how it fell, slid into the furniture, or got accidentally carried into another room.

I enjoy reading mysteries as well. I love the *Encyclopedia Brown* mysteries by Donald J. Sobol, and now that I am a little older, I am starting to read some *Hardy Boys* mysteries by Franklin Dixon and *Nancy Drew* mysteries by Carolyn King. These stories are usually who-done-it mysteries.

A who-done-it is a very popular form of the crime genre. In the who-done-it, the reader is given a list of possible characters and motives and must determine which of the suspects is guilty of the crime. In most cases, a detective is called upon the scene. Two of the greatest detectives in fiction are Hercule Poirot and Miss Marple. These detectives investigated everything from murder to missing jewelry, and, like Alfred Canon's Doyle's Sherlock Holmes, they could crack the most difficult case. Both Hercule Poirot and Miss Marple were created by Agatha.

Agatha's full name was Agatha Mary Clarissa Miller. She was an English woman who wrote mystery stories from 1920 to 1973. In all, she wrote 66 detective novels and fourteen short story collections. She is noted for works such as *Mousetrap* and *Murder on the Orient Express*. Agatha has sold more than two billion copies of her novels, and she holds the Guinness World Record for best-selling fiction writer of all time. Many of her works have been turned into plays.

Agatha believed that if a person thought about things, they could reason through it, and her books are great for challenging one's thinking. She also believed that good advice should always be given, even if it was likely to be ignored – she showed how many times a person was cautioned not to do something and did it anyway only to get hurt. She herself gave lots of advice to budding authors, even if she figured they would ignore it. Her books have consistently received one unfavorable comment – they have a lot of stereotypes. (A stereotype might be a grouchy old man who lives next door.) She herself knew that people were much more complex than a stereotype, but many of her one-dimensional characters do further traditional stereotypes.

Agatha helped popularize the crime genre. I'm guessing you have never heard of Agatha Mary Clarissa Miller. That's because she used two pen names. She wrote six books under the name of Mary Westmacott and the rest under the name . . . **Agatha Christie.**

Moral
Always heed good advice.

44: YOUR NAME SAYS A LOT

Let's play a quick game. I want you to tell me what pops into your mind when you hear the following names: (1) Thomas O'Malley, (2) Bertha, (3) LaDonna, (4) Ling Wong.

If I am guessing, you probably said that Thomas is a Caucasian male, possibly Irish and red-headed, (2) Bertha is Caucasian and likely overweight; (3) LaDonna is African-American, and Ling Wong is Oriental. Want to admit it or not, as soon as we hear a person's name, a stereotype pops up in our mind about their gender, about their race, about how smart they are, and/or about their physical appearance.

Is this fair? No, but it's true. On the first day of school when your teacher receives the class roster, the teacher likely looks at the names and attempts to determine how many of each gender will be in the class. People can't help themselves.

Mary Ann Evans – she was sometimes known as Marian as well – grew up in Victorian England. She knew with the name Mary Anne people would expect writing to be romantic fiction, for that is what women wrote in the 1860s. She, though, wanted to write works that were much more intense than traditional mushy-gushy romantic stories, and so she had to find a pen name. (Believe it or not a lot of writers, singers, and actors still use fake names today.) She knew that women would not buy her books because of how intense they were, and she knew that no man would think that a woman could write as intensely as she could; it's sad, but men didn't respect women writers in her day. She therefore chose to write under the name "George".

She had other reasons for wanting her real name to be a secret as well. The name Mary Ann Evans was widely known in the publishing world as a translator, critic, and editor. If people found out that she was a writer, that might complicate her job. Also, she didn't want her private life to affect how people saw her book; she wanted the book to stand on its own merit. Just like with movie stars today, she had done some embarrassing things that might make people shun her book, so she wanted a name that would be welcomed in all households.

Between 1859 and 1876, she wrote seven novels, the most famous being *Silas Marner* and *Middlemarch.* In her seven books she touched upon the status of women, the state of marriage, and political reform. She knew that social change would not come unless someone planted seeds for it. "If we want to have roses, we must plant roses," she stated, and through her books she sowed the seeds that later women harvested.

The popularity of her novels brought her social acceptance, and, in time, she revealed she was the true author of the works almost everyone was duped into thinking were written by a man: Mary Ann Evans was writing under the name . . . **George Eliot.**

Moral
Plant seeds that you want to see grow.

45: A Deadly Game of Hide and Seek

Have you ever played Hide-and-Seek? In that game, one person closes their eyes and everybody else runs and hides. After counting to an agreed-to number, the person with their eyes closed opens them and starts to look for the people who are hiding. In some versions of the game, the people who are found have to help the one who found them round up the rest of the people; the ones who are hidden, though, are allowed to move from one location to another as long as they are not spotted.

Fourteen year-old Anne and her family were playing Hide-and-Seek, but it wasn't a game. Anne's family was Jewish, and they had moved to the Netherlands when the Nazi Party, which was so anti-Jewish that it literally put Jews to death, came to power. Unfortunately, Adolf Hitler and the Nazis successfully took over the Netherlands, and Anne and her family, like all Jewish families, were sought by the Nazis to be shipped to concentration camps and killed.

The store Anne's dad worked at had a secret apartment built into the back of it. To get into it, one had to remove a bookshelf from the wall inside the store. In July 1942, as the situation worsened for the Jews, Anne's family went into hiding in that apartment. Each day she was in hiding, Anne would write in her journal about events, her thoughts, and her emotions; the journal had been a birthday present. In August 1944, slightly over two years later, the Gestapo found Anne and her family and took them to a series of concentration camps. Anne died of disease in one of the concentration camps the following February.

After the war, her dad returned to Amsterdam and found that his secretary had retrieved Anne's diary. In 1947, he had it published under the title *Diary of a Young Girl*. That work made his daughter one of the most-well-known names of the holocaust, for through that journal she gave people first-hand information of what hiding in the Holocaust was like. She also became an inspiration for anyone facing a hard time. *The Diary of a Young Girl* is still in print today, but it often has a different title today: *The Diary of* . . . **Anne Frank.**

Moral
Face the future with optimism.

46: Retaining the Spirit of Childhood

You don't have to grow up.

That's right, you don't have to grow up. Now, I know your body is changing and that you are getting older with each passing day. I realize that one day you will have a career and likely a family. I even realize that some of you have already had to grow up and take on responsibilities due to circumstances in your family. However, let me say it again – you do not have to grow up.

There is a spirit of childhood. Within that spirit is the joy of imagination. Whereas an adult can see only papers, deadlines, and bills, a person with the spirit of childhood can generate creative solutions to problems. A person with the spirit of childhood can go back into the world of childhood when a niece, nephew, son, or daughter wants to play – and actually enjoy playing "silly" childhood games.

Beatrix had the spirit of childhood. She was an English woman who loved to draw pictures and tell stories. Fortunately for us, she wrote down these stories so that we could enjoy them. She loved animals and the English countryside, so it is no surprise most of her drawings and stories include both of these. She is best known for her stories about Peter Rabbit, Benjamin Bunny, their siblings, and their friends. *The Tale of Peter Rabbit*, written in 1902, is probably the best known of all her stories.

People may tell you to "grow up," but you don't have to leave behind the fun and imagination of childhood. Creativity is not something that only a few have; everybody has the gift of creativity - but many people lose sight of it. In their hurry to "grow up," many people forget about this part of themselves. To recall it, simply take a blank piece of paper and start to write a story – you will be surprised what can come out of your pen. Childhood, creativity, and imagination are not something that we pass through; they are something that we take with us. Whenever you start thinking you are too old to have fun, just think about that senior adult who still could go back to her childhood . . . **Beatrix Potter.**

Moral
Creativity is a gift you have.

47: Harry Potter and the Train Delay

What do you do when you find yourself waiting? Perhaps the dentist was supposed to see you at 2:30pm, but now you find you have a half-hour wait. Perhaps your train was supposed to arrive at 5 p.m., but it is running twenty minutes late. Perhaps your best friend had to go home to eat supper, and now you are sitting by yourself until he comes back.

Waiting is something that we all do. Many of us waste the time. We play on our cell phones or we watch a bland television show. Some of us are more productive, pulling a textbook from our backpack and starting to work on homework.

Joanne, a 25-year-old researcher for Amnesty International, found herself at the Manchester Railroad Station in Manchester, England in 1990. Her train was running late, and, like you and I have had to do so many times, she found herself waiting. As she sat there waiting for the train, a story about a train crossed her mind. That train was the Hogwarts Express.

Who would be getting on that Hogwarts Express train? Why was he getting on? Where was he going? What would happen to him once he got to his destination? Joanne's mind raced to fill in the details. Seven years later, she shared the answers to the questions with the world in the book *Harry Potter and the Philosopher's Stone*. The book did so well that she wrote six sequels to it over the next ten years. These books have since been turned into blockbuster movies.

Joanne became the first author ever to reach billionaire status; she has since given away a large chunk of that money to charity. She has written another book for children, *The Ickabod*, since then, as well as several novels for adults under her own name as well as the private-eye detective series about Cormoran Strike under the name of Robert Galbraith. Her tales of Harry Potter are credited with getting a new generation interested in reading. In the literary world she does not go by Joanne. Her parents named her Joanne Kathleen Rowling; she kept her last name, but she goes by the initials . . . **J. K. Rowling.**

Moral
Make good use of your time.

48: REACH FOR THE TOP

Have you ever picked cherries, pears, apples, oranges, or any other kind of fruit that grows on a tree? From what part of the tree did you pick it? If you are like me – the lady down the street has an apple tree and I've picked fresh apples from it – you probably took the bottom ones. The bottom ones were the easiest to reach.

Sappho was a poet in ancient Greece. She is one of the oldest female poets we have writings of; she may have been about the only female poet in early culture. In those days, writing was something that the leisure class did; most people had to work hard every day to feed themselves. Men were usually the ones with leisure if anyone had it; women were busy baking, cooking, and raising children.

Sappho was from a wealthy family on the island of Lesbos. She wrote over 10,000 pieces; most were to be sung while playing the lyre, a small harp-like instrument. Her works were very, very popular in her time and have remained so throughout history, although most of them have been lost. People nicknamed her "Poetess" and "Tenth Muse".

Sappho was a great poet because she didn't settle for just the low-hanging fruit; she dared to get the ladder and get the jewel at the top. Many people are too lazy to bother with the jewel at the top, so that extra effort is what separates average people from great people. When you think about taking the easy way and doing just enough to get by, remind yourself to reach for the top. It won't be easy, but you'll be rewarded.

Sappho was known as the "Tenth Muse" in her day, so let her be your muse. If you are looking for a complex name, forget it. Like Socrates and Aristotle, two famous Greek men, Sappho didn't have a last name; she was simply . . . **Sappho.**

Moral
Just because it is not easy does not mean it is not worth doing.

49: Never Underestimate the Influence of Friends

Do you and your friends ever have contests?

My friends and I race our bicycles. We all get behind a line and, at the signal, go as fast as we can. Because my friends are trying their hardest, I had to try my hardest. I have to push myself to be better. My friends are setting the standard – and a high one at that – and my goal is to do even better than they are doing.

Mary was a teenage English girl who enjoyed writing. One day, she and her friend, George Byron – he would later be known as Lord Byron, one of England's most famous poets – decided to have a contest to see who could write the best horror story.

History doesn't tell us what George wrote, but the world knows that Mary wrote *Frankenstein*. Fearful that the author being a woman would mean that it would not get published, she published anonymously at age 20. When the book had a solid foothold in society, Mary exposed she was the author on the cover of the second edition.

Frankenstein is the story about a scientist who creates life and then is horrified about what he has done. Many who have not read the book assume that the monster is Frankenstein, but Frankenstein is actually the name of the scientist who built the monster. This book is considered by many people to be one of the first science fiction books ever written.

Mary was the daughter of Mary Wollstonecraft, the feminist who appears in this book as well; her mom died within days of delivering Mary. In addition to being friends with Lord Byron, Mary was married to the poet Percy Bysshe Shelley.

Friends push each other to greatness, and Mary, Percy, and George pushed each other to excellence. (Who knows if any of them would have been great on their own; they all thrived because of those around them.) Later in life, Mary and Percy got married, and Mary even edited Percy's work for him. Choose friends who will inspire you; both Percy and George may owe their career to the inspiration of . . . **Mary Shelley.**

Moral
Choose your friends wisely.

50: She Dared to Put It in Writing

Have you ever tried to set up a club in your backyard with your friends? It's amazing how fast people can shout out ideas. The first time the club meets, the president will keep some sort of order and make sure that all ideas are heard. After some discussion, the club will decide which ideas it wants to accept. After that, the club may do a project or go on an adventure, and then everybody will go home. In the back of their minds, everybody thinks they will remember exactly what was covered at the club.

The next time the club meets, though, have you noticed that people don't remember? Different people recall different things. To remedy this problem, the club president may ask that a club secretary be appointed, and this person will have the duty of writing down the important things the club decides.

Something similar was happening with the women's rights movement that was getting underway in the late 1700s. As different women activists started to speak out about women's rights, it became obvious that they did not agree on what women's rights should look like. Mary saw this problem, and she wanted everyone to be clear about what she thought women's rights should look like; she also did not want anyone to misquote or misinterpret what she said.

She put her thoughts into writing. She wrote *A Vindication of the Rights of Women* in 1792. Now all women could see what she meant, and her ideas would not be taken out of context. The concept of women's rights was foreign to a lot of people – both men and women -in 1792, so having it in writing enabled people to read and think about the reading at their speed.

Mary was a believer in both a woman's innate ability and in education. She believed that if women were given a good education, they could think for themselves and would not have to depend on a man. She believed if women were encouraged to seek accomplishment instead of remaining docile, then they could rise up in society. (As would be expected, some men interpreted this as resulting in a lot of strife in the household, so her writing was very controversial.) As so often happens, her critics dug up muck on her, and focused on the muck instead of encouraging people to think of her ideas. Her ideas, though, did not go away, and her book became the foundation for the women's rights movement. It took a lot of nerve to put it on paper, but that is what was needed. Today, the founder of the women's rights movement is generally considered to be . . . **Mary Wollstonecraft.**

Moral
Don't trust your memory for important details; put it in writing.

51: We Women have Something to Say

Have you ever held up your hand in class to answer a question, but the teacher didn't call on you? It was frustrating, wasn't it?

What did you do? Did you pound on the desk with your other hand to get the teacher's attention? Did you start to grunt or whisper, "Me. Me. Pick me," or excitedly call, "I know. I know"? Did you simply put your hand down in discouragement? Did you finally just blurt out the answer?

Women writers have had things to say for centuries, but society refused to acknowledge their voice. It was as if they had their hands up, but the teacher didn't want to hear what they had to say. Virginia was a woman writer in the early 1900s in England, and she was having the same trouble.

Virginia realized women writers had struggled for years to be heard, and they had followed all the techniques suggested above. Some had sent their work to the editor in hopes of being published, and the editors had turned down their work. Some had submitted their work anonymously or with a male pen name, and they had gotten their voice heard but they had not received the credit. Some had found their way around traditional publishers and had dared to simply blurt out what they had to say by printing it themselves – Virginia chose the latter way.

Virginia's husband owned a printing company, and he would publish her work for her. She got her message out, the message that women could write. In fact, Virginia not only wrote novels, she took novel writing in a new direction, introducing the stream-of-consciousness narrator. (With this type of narrator, you learn every thought that is going through the person's mind; it makes for a fascinating but slightly disjointed – we all get distracted by squirrels – reading experience. Virginia's most famous books are *Mrs. Dalloway* and *To the Lighthouse*.

Virginia was living proof that women could be writers. Virginia wanted to do more, though, for the women's movement than just be a subtle example. Therefore, she became very open about women's rights. She directly advanced the women's movement by writing, *A Room of One's Own* and *Three Guineas*. Like the wolf in the story The Three Little Pigs, she was huffing, and puffing, and going to blow down the house of inequality; that metaphor makes her name easy for me to remember; she's . . . Virginia Woolf.

Moral
Find a way to say what needs to be said.

Part V

ENTERTAINERS AND ATHLETES

52: The Supercalifragilisticexpialidocious Actress

Have you ever been camping? If you haven't, and you get the opportunity to go, take it. When a person goes camping, a person becomes one with nature. When we go camping, my dad makes sure that everything is left just like we found it. In fact, he does even more – he makes sure it is better than the way we found it. If there is litter from a previous camper, he will ask that we pick it up. He wants us to learn that no matter where we go or what we do, we should be making the place better than it was before we got there.

Julia Wells shared that same optimism as my dad on stage and off. She was an English actress with a beautiful four-octave voice. Having starred in some musicals on Broadway, she was selected to play the nanny Mary Poppins in *Mary Poppins*, and, later, the lead role in *the Sound of Music*. These roles won her fans around the globe. During her career, she won a British Academy Film Award, one Academy Award, two Emmy Awards, and three Grammy Awards, and the American Film Institute's (AFI) Lifetime Achievement Award.

In 1997, the unthinkable happened – she had an operation and things didn't go right. The operation damaged her vocal cords; she could not sing. What would an optimistic person do in a situation like this? Become a pessimist?

Not Julia. She might not be able to sing like she used to do, but she could still speak. Julia took on speaking roles, including Queen Lillian in the *Shrek* movie series and the sea monster in *Aquaman*. She also took on acting roles, starring in such movies as *The Princess Diaries* and *The Princess Diaries II*. Julia knew there were still opportunities out there, and she wasn't going to miss them feeling sorry for herself.

Julia wanted to make the world a better place for her having been in it. Even in her films, if someone was down, she tried to cheer them up. For instance, in *Mary Poppins*, when the two children in her care were scared and shy, she taught them a new word that would always make them laugh - supercalifragilisticexpialidocious, which means "wonderful". She also likely informed them of her stage name . . . **Julie Andrews.**

Moral
Seek to make the world a better place one small deed at a time.

53: Tough Emotionally; Tough Physically

What inspires you to get up every morning?

Do you do it because you want to please your mom? Do you do it because the state law says that you must attend school until you are at least sixteen? Do you do it because you know that if you finish this year and a few more, you will likely get a good job? Do you do it because your dad promised you twenty dollars if you got a good grade in a tough subject?

All of those are good reasons, but, sooner or later, they will not work anymore. One day you will be sixteen, and don't have to risk punishment if you don't go to school. One day you will have all the money that you need to be happy; you'll likely turn down more money to spend time with your family. The very best reason for doing something is "because you want to do it."

Joanna is a Mixed Martial Artist; that is, she fights other girls for a living in an almost-anything-goes style match. Joanna knows of lots of reasons to get into that cage to fight – some people do it for the money, some for the glamour, and some for the fame, but she knows all of those are fleeting. She gets in the cage because she wants to do it; she wants to be the very best fighter she can be. Internal drive is the secret to her success.

Joanna is from Poland and currently competes in the Strawweight Division of the Ultimate Fighting Championship (UFC). She is the former champion of that division. Joanna has offered her own life as an example for other women in terms of both fitness and inspiration. Although she doesn't go into a lot of details, she admits that her boyfriend cheated on her and that her manager stole money from her; she overcame both setbacks. If anyone thinks that all girls are frail and fragile, either physically or emotionally, she encourages them to look at the life of . . . **Joanna Jedrzejczyk.**

Moral
Find internal motivation.

54: Tennis, Anyone?

Have you ever had one of those days when nobody wants to play with you? I think we all have.

Seven-year-old Martina loved to play tennis. She was good at it too, but she wanted to get better. To get better, she needed to practice. To practice, she needed someone to play against. The old saying that "iron sharpens iron" was true, and if no one would play against her, then she could not get better.

Or could she? The first few statements were true. She did love tennis. She was good at tennis. She wanted to get better at tennis. She needed to practice. All of those were true. However, the next statement, she realized, was not - she did not need somebody to play against. She could hit the tennis ball against a concrete wall.

If you want something bad enough, you will find a way to do it. Martina could have quit, and no one would have blamed her – after, there was no one around to practice with. However, she did not quit. Instead, she practiced, and she got better and better. In 2006, *Tennis* magazine identified her as the greatest female tennis player for the years 1975 – 2005. She is the only person in tennis history to have been number one for over 200 consecutive weeks in both singles and doubles – she had 237 weeks at number one in doubles (a record) and 332 weeks at number one in singles (a record that is second only to Steffi Graf's 377 weeks).

She was born in Prague, Czechoslovakia and became an American citizen in 1981; she has dual citizenship today. In 1981, Martina announced that she is bisexual, and in 2014 she proposed to her long-time girlfriend at the U.S. Open. (The two were married later that year.)

After retiring from professional tennis, Martina has tried her hand at writing mysteries, books about her life as a tennis star, and a cookbook. Although she is venturing into new fields, her public identity remains in tennis. She is a role model for girls around the world, showing them that they can do what appears to be the impossible. Whenever something looks hopeless, keep believing in yourself, keep asking how you can achieve the result you want, and think about that brick wall. When people see a brick wall, they tend to turn around in disappointment; when Martina saw a concrete wall, she saw opportunity. She made the wall her ally; that wall exchanged tennis volleys with . . . **Martina Navratilova.**

Moral
Believe in yourself.

55: The Dying Swan

Have you ever used a symbol?

A symbol is an item that stands for something else. For instance, a red, white, and blue flag with 50 stars on it represents the United States of America in 2021. It is often used in pictures of the President of the United States to show that he is ruler of the country. It is also used to suggest patriotism and to show Americans are present. (Did you know that in 1969 the astronauts intentionally left an American flag on the moon?)

Anna was a Russian ballet dancer. To her, dancing was not just about exercise. Nor was it about being graceful. She saw dance as a way of expressing things when words could not express them.

Anna began her career with the Imperial Ballet in 1891 at age ten; in 1911, she set up her own ballet company. She toured the world with her company, becoming the first ballerina to ever tour the world. She went to the United States, South America, Australia, and India, to name just a few of the places. Anna was especially known for "The Swan," a dance that she created in 1905. The four-minute dance told the life story of a swan, including its dying day. The dance was later renamed "The Dying Swan," for the entire dance led to that climatic moment of death. The swan was a symbol for one's own life, and people grasped the symbolism.

Women weren't supposed to travel the world, they weren't supposed to own their own company, and they weren't encouraged to express themselves in the arts. Anna ignored traditional roles and sought to share emotions that could not be captured by words. Everywhere she went, she inspired other people to fall in love with ballet. Both girls and boys became interested in becoming performers, and many who thought they hated ballet realized they actually enjoyed it when it was done right. Her performances were so moving that she often brought audiences to tears. Although not everyone in the audience spoke Russian, they all recognized the grace and the symbolism in her performances.

Anna was an inspiration to women (and men) around the world in more ways than one. She was literally a woman who was on her toes; she showed that when hard work was added to one's talent, genius could result. "The Dying Swan" has since been reinterpreted by other dancers since then. To see the original as Anna intended it, you would have to catch the dance being performed by . . . **Anna Pavlova.**

Moral
Expression does not have to be by words or writing, dance can work as well.

Did you enjoy the book?

If you did, we are ecstatic. If not, please write your complaint to us and we will ensure we fix it.

If you're feeling generous, there is something important that you can help me with – tell other people that you enjoyed the book.

Ask a grown-up to write about it on Amazon. When they do, more people will find out about the book. It also lets Amazon know that we are making kids around the world learn. Even a few words and ratings would go a long way.

If you have any ideas or jokes that you think are super funny, please let us know. We would love to hear from you. Our email address is -

riddleland@riddlelandforkids.com

Other Fun Books By Riddleland Riddles Series

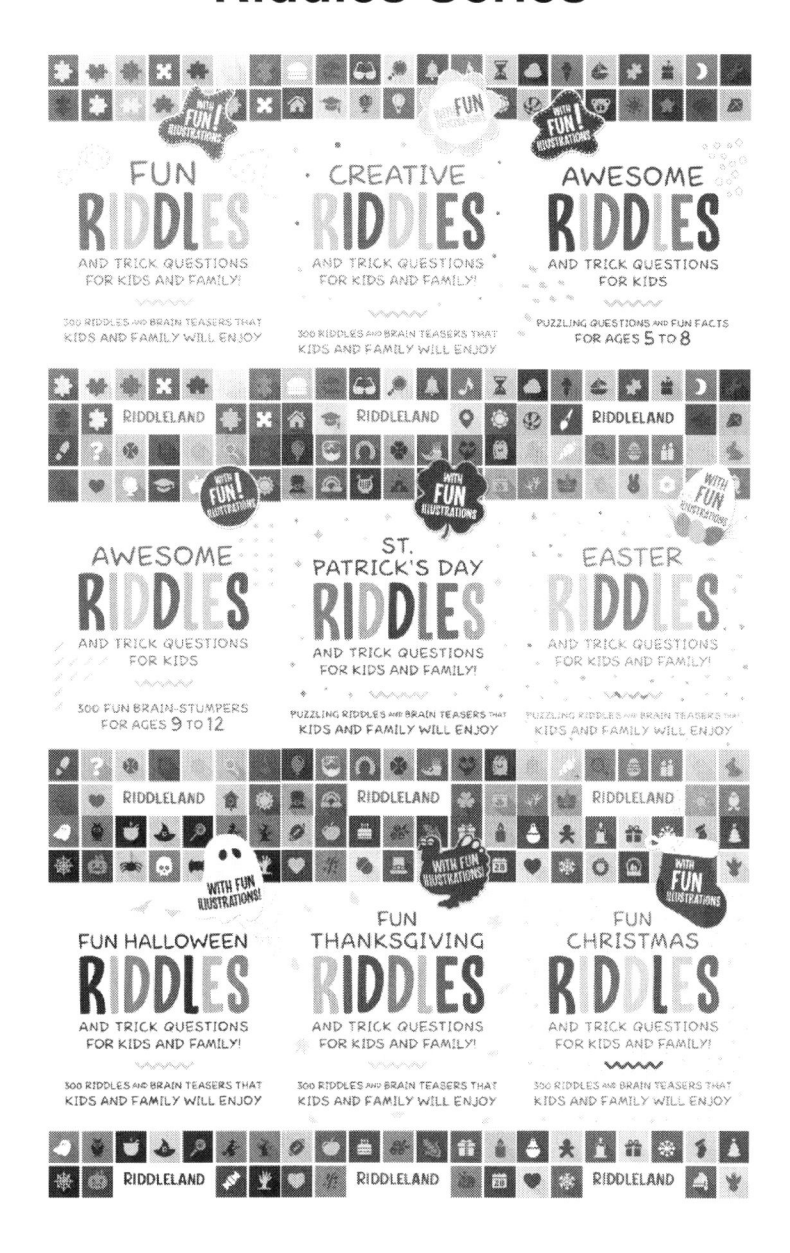

Fun Riddles
And Trick Questions For Kids And Family!
300 Riddles and Brain Teasers That Kids and Family Will Enjoy

Creative Riddles
And Trick Questions For Kids And Family!
300 Riddles and Brain Teasers That Kids and Family Will Enjoy

Awesome Riddles
And Trick Questions For Kids
Puzzling Questions and Fun Facts For Ages 5 to 8

Awesome Riddles
And Trick Questions For Kids
300 Fun Brain-Stumpers For Ages 9 to 12

St. Patrick's Day Riddles
And Trick Questions For Kids And Family!
Puzzling Riddles and Brain Teasers That Kids and Family Will Enjoy

Easter Riddles
And Trick Questions For Kids And Family!
Puzzling Riddles and Brain Teasers That Kids and Family Will Enjoy

Fun Halloween Riddles
And Trick Questions For Kids And Family!
300 Riddles and Brain Teasers That Kids and Family Will Enjoy

Fun Thanksgiving Riddles
And Trick Questions For Kids And Family!
300 Riddles and Brain Teasers That Kids and Family Will Enjoy

Fun Christmas Riddles
And Trick Questions For Kids And Family!
300 Riddles and Brain Teasers That Kids and Family Will Enjoy

Its Laugh O'Clock Joke Books

It's Laugh O'Clock Would You Rather Books

Get them on Amazon
or our website at www.riddlelandforkids.com

About Riddleland

Riddleland is a mum + dad run publishing company. We are passionate about creating fun and innovative books to help children develop their reading skills and fall in love with reading. If you have suggestions for us or want to work with us, shoot us an email at

riddleland@riddlelandforkids.com

Our family's favorite quote:

"Creativity is an area in which younger people
have a tremendous advantage since
they have an endearing habit of always
questioning past wisdom and authority."
~ Bill Hewlett

REFERENCES

10 facts ON CIXI - the Empress who ushered in Modern China. (n.d.). Retrieved June 17, 2021, from https://www.chinahighlights.com/travelguide/china-history/empress-cixi-facts.htm

21 of the best quotes By Valentina Tereshkova. (n.d.). Retrieved June 17, 2021, from https://www.quoteikon.com/valentina-tereshkova-quotes.html

700 quotes BY JANE Austen [PAGE - 2]: A-Z Quotes. (n.d.). Retrieved June 18, 2021, from https://www.azquotes.com/author/669-Jane_Austen?p=2

Ada Lovelace. (2021, June 15). Retrieved June 17, 2021, from https://en.wikipedia.org/wiki/Ada_Lovelace

Agatha Christie bibliography. (2021, May 01). Retrieved June 18, 2021, from https://en.wikipedia.org/wiki/Agatha_Christie_bibliography

Agatha Christie. (2021, June 12). Retrieved June 18, 2021, from https://en.wikipedia.org/wiki/Agatha_Christie

Alvsa, Z. (2021, June 03). 30 powerful Joanna Jedrzejczyk quotes. Retrieved June 18, 2021, from https://wealthygorilla.com/joanna-jedrzejczyk-quotes/

Angela Merkel quotes about Democracy: A-Z Quotes. (n.d.). Retrieved June 17, 2021, from https://www.azquotes.com/author/9995-Angela_Merkel/tag/democracy

Angela Merkel. (2020, March 23). Retrieved June 17, 2021, from https://www.biography.com/political-figure/angela-merkel

Angela Merkel. (2021, June 16). Retrieved June 17, 2021, from https://en.wikipedia.org/wiki/Angela_Merkel

Anita Roddick. (2008, October 10). Retrieved June 17, 2021, from https://www.entrepreneur.com/article/197688

Anita Roddick. (2021, June 01). Retrieved June 17, 2021, from https://en.wikipedia.org/wiki/Anita_Roddick

Anna Pavlova. (2021, March 26). Retrieved June 18, 2021, from https://www.biography.com/performer/anna-pavlova

Anna Pavlova. (2021, May 21). Retrieved June 18, 2021, from https://en.wikipedia.org/wiki/Anna_Pavlova

Anne Boleyn. (2020, March 02). Retrieved June 17, 2021, from https://www.biography.com/royalty/anne-boleyn

Anne Boleyn. (2021, June 08). Retrieved June 17, 2021, from https://en.wikipedia.org/wiki/Anne_Boleyn

Anne Frank. (2021, June 03). Retrieved June 18, 2021, from https://en.wikipedia.org/wiki/Anne_Frank

Apartheid. (2021, June 16). Retrieved June 17, 2021, from https://en.wikipedia.org/wiki/Apartheid

Beatrix Potter Quotes (author of the tale of Peter rabbit). (n.d.). Retrieved June 18, 2021, from https://www.goodreads.com/author/quotes/11593.Beatrix_Potter

Beatrix Potter. (2021, April 22). Retrieved June 18, 2021, from https://www.biography.com/writer/beatrix-potter

Beatrix Potter. (2021, June 06). Retrieved June 18, 2021, from https://en.wikipedia.org/wiki/Beatrix_Potter

Benazir Bhutto. (2021, April 22). Retrieved June 17, 2021, from https://www.biography.com/political-figure/benazir-bhutto

Benazir Bhutto. (2021, June 15). Retrieved June 17, 2021, from https://en.wikipedia.org/wiki/Benazir_Bhutto

Best mary shelley quotes. (n.d.). Retrieved June 18, 2021, from https://quotes.thefamouspeople.com/mary-shelley-2302.php

Betty Williams (peace activist). (2021, May 28). Retrieved June 17, 2021, from https://en.wikipedia.org/wiki/Betty_Williams_(peace_activist)

Biography. (n.d.). Retrieved June 17, 2021, from https://motherteresa.org/biography.html

Calico Jack. (2021, June 14). Retrieved June 17, 2021, from https://en.wikipedia.org/wiki/Calico_Jack

Catherine de' Medici Quotes. (n.d.). Retrieved June 17, 2021, from https://libquotes.com/catherine-de-medici

Catherine the great. (2021, June 08). Retrieved June 17, 2021, from https://en.wikipedia.org/wiki/Catherine_the_Great

Changed the Game: Junko Tabei, the first woman to ASCEND EVEREST, quietly moved mountains for women's rights. (n.d.). Retrieved June 17, 2021, from https://www.msn.com/en-us/news/world/changed-the-game-junko-tabei-the-first-woman-to-ascend-everest-quietly-moved-mountains-for-womens-rights/ar-BB1ew969

Charlotte Brontë. (2021, April 13). Retrieved June 18, 2021, from https://www.biography.com/writer/charlotte-bronte

Charlotte Brontë. (2021, June 17). Retrieved June 18, 2021, from https://en.wikipedia.org/wiki/Charlotte_Bront%C3%AB

Christopher Columbus. (2021, March 29). Retrieved June 17, 2021, from https://www.biography.com/explorer/christopher-columbus

Cixi. (n.d.). Retrieved June 17, 2021, from https://www.britannica.com/biography/Cixi

Cleopatra facts for kids. (n.d.). Retrieved June 17, 2021, from https://kids.kiddle.co/Cleopatra

Cleopatra. (2021, June 16). Retrieved June 17, 2021, from https://en.wikipedia.org/wiki/Cleopatra

Coco Chanel. (2021, April 09). Retrieved June 17, 2021, from https://www.biography.com/fashion-designer/coco-chanel

Coco Chanel. (2021, June 14). Retrieved June 17, 2021, from https://en.wikipedia.org/wiki/Coco_Chanel

Coppens, T. (2012, September 04). Quotations from real pirates. Retrieved June 17, 2021, from https://owlcation.com/humanities/Quotations-from-Real-Pirates

Diana, Princess of Wales. (2021, June 14). Retrieved June 17, 2021, from https://en.wikipedia.org/wiki/Diana,_Princess_of_Wales

Did Marie-Antoinette really say "let them eat cake"? (n.d.). Retrieved June 17, 2021, from https://www.britannica.com/story/did-marie-antoinette-really-say-let-them-eat-cake

The dying swan. (2021, April 06). Retrieved June 18, 2021, from https://en.wikipedia.org/wiki/The_Dying_Swan

Elizabeth Blackwell. (2021, June 11). Retrieved June 17, 2021, from https://en.wikipedia.org/wiki/Elizabeth_Blackwell

Elizabeth Blackwell. (2021, March 31). Retrieved June 17, 2021, from https://www.biography.com/scientist/elizabeth-blackwell

Elizabeth Fry History. (n.d.). Retrieved June 17, 2021, from https://www.elizabethfry.co.uk/History

Elizabeth fry. (2021, June 08). Retrieved June 17, 2021, from https://en.wikipedia.org/wiki/Elizabeth_Fry

Elizabeth Garrett Anderson. (2021, May 06). Retrieved June 17, 2021, from https://en.wikipedia.org/wiki/Elizabeth_Garrett_Anderson

Elizabeth Garrett Anderson: First woman doctor in Britain and her biography. (n.d.). Retrieved June 17, 2021, from https://victorian-era.org/elizabeth-garrett-anderson.html

Elizabeth I of England. (2020, June 02). Retrieved June 17, 2021, from https://en.wikipedia.org/wiki/Elizabeth_I_of_England

Elizabeth II. (2021, June 15). Retrieved June 17, 2021, from https://en.wikipedia.org/wiki/Elizabeth_II

Emmeline Pankhurst. (2021, June 10). Retrieved June 17, 2021, from https://en.wikipedia.org/wiki/Emmeline_Pankhurst

Empress Dowager Cixi (4 Sourced QUOTES). (n.d.). Retrieved June 17, 2021, from https://libquotes.com/empress-dowager-cixi

Empress Dowager Cixi. (2021, May 28). Retrieved June 17, 2021, from https://en.wikipedia.org/wiki/Empress_Dowager_Cixi

European Union. (2021, June 16). Retrieved June 17, 2021, from https://en.wikipedia.org/wiki/European_Union
The female soldier. (n.d.). Retrieved June 17, 2021, from http://thefemalesoldier.com/blog/tag/female+pirates

Florence Nightingale. (2021, June 08). Retrieved June 17, 2021, from https://en.wikipedia.org/wiki/Florence_Nightingale

Frankenstein. (2021, June 15). Retrieved June 18, 2021, from https://en.wikipedia.org/wiki/Frankenstein

George Eliot Quotes (author of Middlemarch). (n.d.). Retrieved June 18, 2021, from https://www.goodreads.com/author/quotes/173.George_Eliot

George Eliot. (2021, May 31). Retrieved June 18, 2021, from https://en.wikipedia.org/wiki/George_Eliot

Golda Meir. (2021, April 20). Retrieved June 17, 2021, from https://www.biography.com/political-figure/golda-meir

Golda Meir. (2021, June 11). Retrieved June 17, 2021, from https://en.wikipedia.org/wiki/Golda_Meir

Greta Thunberg. (2021, June 14). Retrieved June 17, 2021, from https://en.wikipedia.org/wiki/Greta_Thunberg

Hendricks, J. (2020, January 10). UFC star Joanna jedrzejczyk's Downfall: 'cheating' fiancé, stealing manager. Retrieved June 18, 2021, from https://nypost.com/2020/01/10/ufc-star-joanna-jedrzejczyks-downfall-cheating-fiance-stealing-manager/

History - george eliot. (n.d.). Retrieved June 18, 2021, from http://www.bbc.co.uk/history/historic_figures/eliot_george.shtml

History - josephine butler. (n.d.). Retrieved June 17, 2021, from http://www.bbc.co.uk/history/historic_figures/butler_josephine.shtml

History.com Editors. (2009, November 09). Anne Frank. Retrieved June 18, 2021, from https://www.history.com/topics/world-war-ii/anne-frank-1

History.com Editors. (2009, November 09). Florence Nightingale. Retrieved June 17, 2021, from https://www.history.com/topics/womens-history/florence-nightingale-1

History.com Editors. (2009, November 09). Joan of Arc. Retrieved June 17, 2021, from https://www.history.com/topics/middle-ages/saint-joan-of-arc

History.com Editors. (2019, May 15). Irish Republican Army: Timeline. Retrieved June 17, 2021, from https://www.history.com/topics/21st-century/irish-republican-army

Hoon, S. (2020, November 01). Best anna pavlova quotes and achievements. Retrieved June 18, 2021, from https://danceivy.com/blogs/news/best-anna-pavlova-quotes-and-achievements

Hundred years' War. (2021, June 07). Retrieved June 17, 2021, from https://en.wikipedia.org/wiki/Hundred_Years%27_War

Indira Gandhi. (2021, June 11). Retrieved June 17, 2021, from https://en.wikipedia.org/wiki/Indira_Gandhi

Isabella I of Castile. (2021, June 05). Retrieved June 17, 2021, from https://en.wikipedia.org/wiki/Isabella_I_of_Castile

Isabella I. (n.d.). Retrieved June 17, 2021, from https://biography.yourdictionary.com/isabella-i

J. (2020, November 11). 30 greatest Florence Nightingale quotes for nurses. Retrieved June 17, 2021, from https://www.nursebuff.com/florence-nightingale-quotes/

J. K. Rowling. (2021, June 14). Retrieved June 18, 2021, from https://en.wikipedia.org/wiki/J._K._Rowling

J.K. Rowling. (n.d.). Retrieved June 18, 2021, from https://www.britannica.com/biography/J-K-Rowling

Jane Austen. (2021, May 06). Retrieved June 18, 2021, from https://www.biography.com/writer/jane-austen

Jane Austen. (2021, May 30). Retrieved June 18, 2021, from https://en.wikipedia.org/wiki/Jane_Austen

Jane Eyre. (2021, June 16). Retrieved June 18, 2021, from https://en.wikipedia.org/wiki/Jane_Eyre

Jane Goodall. (2021, June 03). Retrieved June 17, 2021, from https://en.wikipedia.org/wiki/Jane_Goodall

Jane Goodall. (2021, May 06). Retrieved June 17, 2021, from https://www.biography.com/scientist/jane-goodall

Joan of Arc. (2021, June 01). Retrieved June 17, 2021, from https://en.wikipedia.org/wiki/Joan_of_Arc

Joanna jedrzejczyk. (2020, March 07). Retrieved June 18, 2021, from https://www.ufc.com/athlete/joanna-jedrzejczyk

Joanna Jędrzejczyk. (2021, May 25). Retrieved June 18, 2021, from https://en.wikipedia.org/wiki/Joanna_J%C4%99drzejczyk

Josephine Butler BIOGRAPHY, Life, interesting facts. (n.d.). Retrieved June 17, 2021, from https://www.sunsigns.org/famousbirthdays/profile/josephine-butler/

Josephine Butler. (2018, August 24). Retrieved June 17, 2021, from https://en.wikiquote.org/wiki/Josephine_Butler

Julie Andrews. (2021, February 05). Retrieved June 18, 2021, from https://www.biography.com/actor/julie-andrews

Julie Andrews. (2021, June 16). Retrieved June 18, 2021, from https://en.wikipedia.org/wiki/Julie_Andrews

Julie Andrews. (n.d.). Retrieved June 18, 2021, from https://www.britannica.com/biography/Julie-Andrews

Junko Tabei. (2021, May 16). Retrieved June 17, 2021, from https://en.wikipedia.org/wiki/Junko_Tabei

Kettler, S. (2020, June 17). Emmeline Pankhurst. Retrieved June 17, 2021, from https://www.biography.com/activist/emmeline-pankhurst

Langer, E. (2020, March 25). Betty Williams, Nobel laureate and leader of peace movement in Northern Ireland, dies at 76. Retrieved June 17, 2021, from https://www.washingtonpost.com/local/obituaries/betty-williams-nobel-laureate-and-leader-of-peace-movement-in-northern-ireland-dies-at-76/2020/03/23/d9010784-6a9d-11ea-abef-020f086a3fab_story.html

Lewis, J. (n.d.). Biography of Catherine the Great, Empress of Russia. Retrieved June 17, 2021, from https://www.thoughtco.com/catherine-the-great-p2-3528624

Margaret Thatcher. (2020, December 02). Retrieved June 17, 2021, from https://www.biography.com/political-figure/margaret-thatcher

Margaret Thatcher. (2021, June 16). Retrieved June 17, 2021, from https://en.wikipedia.org/wiki/Margaret_Thatcher

Maria Bochkareva. (2021, April 06). Retrieved June 17, 2021, from https://en.wikipedia.org/wiki/Maria_Bochkareva

Marie Antoinette. (2021, June 14). Retrieved June 17, 2021, from https://en.wikipedia.org/wiki/Marie_Antoinette

Marie Curie. (2021, April 09). Retrieved June 17, 2021, from https://www.biography.com/scientist/marie-curie

Marie Curie. (2021, June 13). Retrieved June 17, 2021, from https://en.wikipedia.org/wiki/Marie_Curie

Marie-Antoinette. (n.d.). Retrieved June 17, 2021, from https://www.britannica.com/biography/Marie-Antoinette-queen-of-France

Martina Navratilova BIOGRAPHY, Life, interesting facts. (n.d.). Retrieved June 18, 2021, from https://www.sunsigns.org/famousbirthdays/profile/martina-navratilova/

Martina Navratilova. (2021, June 16). Retrieved June 18, 2021, from https://en.wikipedia.org/wiki/Martina_Navratilova

Mary I if England. (n.d.). Retrieved June 17, 2021, from https://quotes.yourdictionary.com/author/mary-i-of-england/82177 Mary I of England. (2021, June 11). Retrieved June 17, 2021, from https://en.wikipedia.org/wiki/Mary_I_of_England Mary read Biography. (n.d.). Retrieved June 17, 2021, from http://www.famous-pirates.com/famous-pirates/mary-read/

Mary read. (2021, May 28). Retrieved June 17, 2021, from https://en.wikipedia.org/wiki/Mary_Read

Mary Shelley. (2021, June 05). Retrieved June 18, 2021, from https://en.wikipedia.org/wiki/Mary_Shelley

Mary Shelley. (2021, May 06). Retrieved June 18, 2021, from https://www.biography.com/writer/mary-shelley

Mary Tudor. (2021, May 06). Retrieved June 17, 2021, from https://www.biography.com/royalty/mary-tudor

Mary Wollstonecraft. (2021, May 06). Retrieved June 18, 2021, from https://www.biography.com/scholar/mary-wollstonecraft

Mary Wollstonecraft. (2021, May 19). Retrieved June 18, 2021, from https://en.wikipedia.org/wiki/Mary_Wollstonecraft

McIlvenna, U. (2018, October 25). What inspired queen 'bloody' mary's gruesome nickname? Retrieved June 17, 2021, from https://www.history.com/news/queen-mary-i-bloody-mary-reformation

Mother Teresa. (2021, June 14). Retrieved June 17, 2021, from https://en.wikipedia.org/wiki/Mother_Teresa

Nix, E. (2016, February 16). 8 things you might not know about Mary I. Retrieved June 17, 2021, from https://www.history.com/news/8-things-you-might-not-know-about-mary-i

Nowak, C. (2021, June 11). The 26 most inspiring quotes from Princess Diana. Retrieved June 17, 2021, from https://www.rd.com/list/princess-diana-quotes/

Olushola. (2018, April 03). 10 memorable quotes of Winnie Mandela. Retrieved June 17, 2021, from https://punchng.com/10-memorable-quotes-of-winnie-mandela/

Prahl, A. (n.d.). The life and reign of Catherine de MEDICI, Renaissance Queen. Retrieved June 17, 2021, from https://www.thoughtco.com/catherine-de-medici-biography-4155305

Princess Diana. (2021, June 03). Retrieved June 17, 2021, from https://www.biography.com/royalty/princess-diana

Queen Elizabeth I. (2020, February 07). Retrieved June 17, 2021, from https://www.biography.com/royalty/queen-elizabeth-i

Queen Elizabeth II. (2021, April 09). Retrieved June 17, 2021, from https://www.biography.com/royalty/queen-elizabeth-ii
Queen Isabella of SPAIN facts: The BIOGRAPHY QUOTES. (n.d.). Retrieved June 17, 2021, from https://elizabethanenglandlife.com/thetudorsfacts/queen-isabella-of-spain-facts-biography-quotes-timeline-and-accomplishments.html

Queen Victoria i's DETAILED biography. Parents, childhood and death. (n.d.). Retrieved June 17, 2021, from http://victorian-era.org/queen-victorias-biography-facts.html

Queen Victoria. (2021, June 11). Retrieved June 17, 2021, from https://en.wikipedia.org/wiki/Queen_Victoria

Rae, C. (2015, April 20). Maria Bochkareva. Retrieved June 17, 2021, from http://thefemalesoldier.com/blog/maria-bochkareva

Rosa Luxemburg facts for kids. (n.d.). Retrieved June 17, 2021, from https://kids.kiddle.co/Rosa_Luxemburg

Rosa Luxemburg. (2021, June 10). Retrieved June 17, 2021, from https://en.wikipedia.org/wiki/Rosa_Luxemburg

Rosa Luxemburg. (n.d.). Retrieved June 17, 2021, from https://kids.britannica.com/students/article/Rosa-Luxemburg/275561

Rosalind Franklin Quotes (author Of HerStory). (n.d.). Retrieved June 17, 2021, from https://www.goodreads.com/author/quotes/232917.Rosalind_Franklin

Rosalind Franklin. (2020, June 15). Retrieved June 17, 2021, from https://www.biography.com/scientist/rosalind-franklin

Rosalind Franklin. (2021, June 15). Retrieved June 17, 2021, from https://en.wikipedia.org/wiki/Rosalind_Franklin

Sappho. (2021, June 08). Retrieved June 18, 2021, from https://en.wikipedia.org/wiki/Sappho

Sappho. (n.d.). Retrieved June 18, 2021, from https://www.britannica.com/biography/Sappho-Greek-poet

Simkin, J. (n.d.). Spartacus educational. Retrieved June 17, 2021, from https://spartacus-educational.com/FWWbochkareva.htm

Spartacist uprising. (2021, May 19). Retrieved June 17, 2021, from https://en.wikipedia.org/wiki/Spartacist_uprising

St Bartholomews Day massacre. (2008, October 08). Retrieved June 17, 2021, from https://en.wikipedia.org/wiki/St_Bartholomews_day_Massacre

Svoboda, M. (n.d.). Sappho quotes (15 Quotes): Quotes of famous people. Retrieved June 18, 2021, from https://quotepark.com/authors/sappho/

Szczepanski, K. (n.d.). Biography of empress Cixi, the Dragon Lady of Late Qing China. Retrieved June 17, 2021, from https://www.thoughtco.com/cixi-empress-dowager-of-qing-china-195615

Valentina Tereshkova. (2021, June 09). Retrieved June 17, 2021, from https://en.wikipedia.org/wiki/Valentina_Tereshkova

Valentina Tereshkova. (2021, May 25). Retrieved June 17, 2021, from https://www.biography.com/astronaut/valentina-tereshkova

Virginia Woolf. (2020, March 27). Retrieved June 18, 2021, from https://www.biography.com/writer/virginia-woolf

Virginia Woolf. (2021, June 10). Retrieved June 18, 2021, from https://en.wikipedia.org/wiki/Virginia_Woolf

Wangari Maathai. (2020, July 07). Retrieved June 17, 2021, from https://www.biography.com/activist/wangari-maathai Wangari Maathai. (2021, May 17). Retrieved June 17, 2021, from https://en.wikipedia.org/wiki/Wangari_Maathai

Who is Greta THUNBERG? Everything you need to know. (n.d.). Retrieved June 17, 2021, from https://www.thefamouspeople.com/profiles/greta-thunberg-47896.php

Who was Ada LOVELACE? Everything you need to know. (n.d.). Retrieved June 17, 2021, from https://www.thefamouspeople.com/profiles/ada-lovelace-6234.php

Who was Mary Wollstonecraft? Everything you need to know. (n.d.). Retrieved June 18, 2021, from https://www.thefamouspeople.com/profiles/mary-wollstonecraft-2304.php

Winnie madikizela-mandela. (2021, June 14). Retrieved June 17, 2021, from https://en.wikipedia.org/wiki/Winnie_ Madikizela-Mandela

Written ByPaul Davies Paul works for a helpdesk software company and is one of the co-founders of Curious Earth. (2021, April 14). 29 of GRETA THUNBERG'S best quotes - Curious EARTH: Climate change. Retrieved June 17, 2021, from https://curious.earth/blog/greta-thunberg-quotes-best-21/

Yom Kippur War. (2021, June 14). Retrieved June 17, 2021, from https://en.wikipedia.org/wiki/Yom_Kippur_War

Вадим, С. (2013, September 16). Russian Jeanne d'Arc Maria BOCHKAREVA and her FEMALE "death battalion". Retrieved June 17, 2021, from https://en.topwar.ru/33211-russkaya-zhanna-dark-mariya-bochkareva-i-ee-zhenskiy-batalon-smerti.html